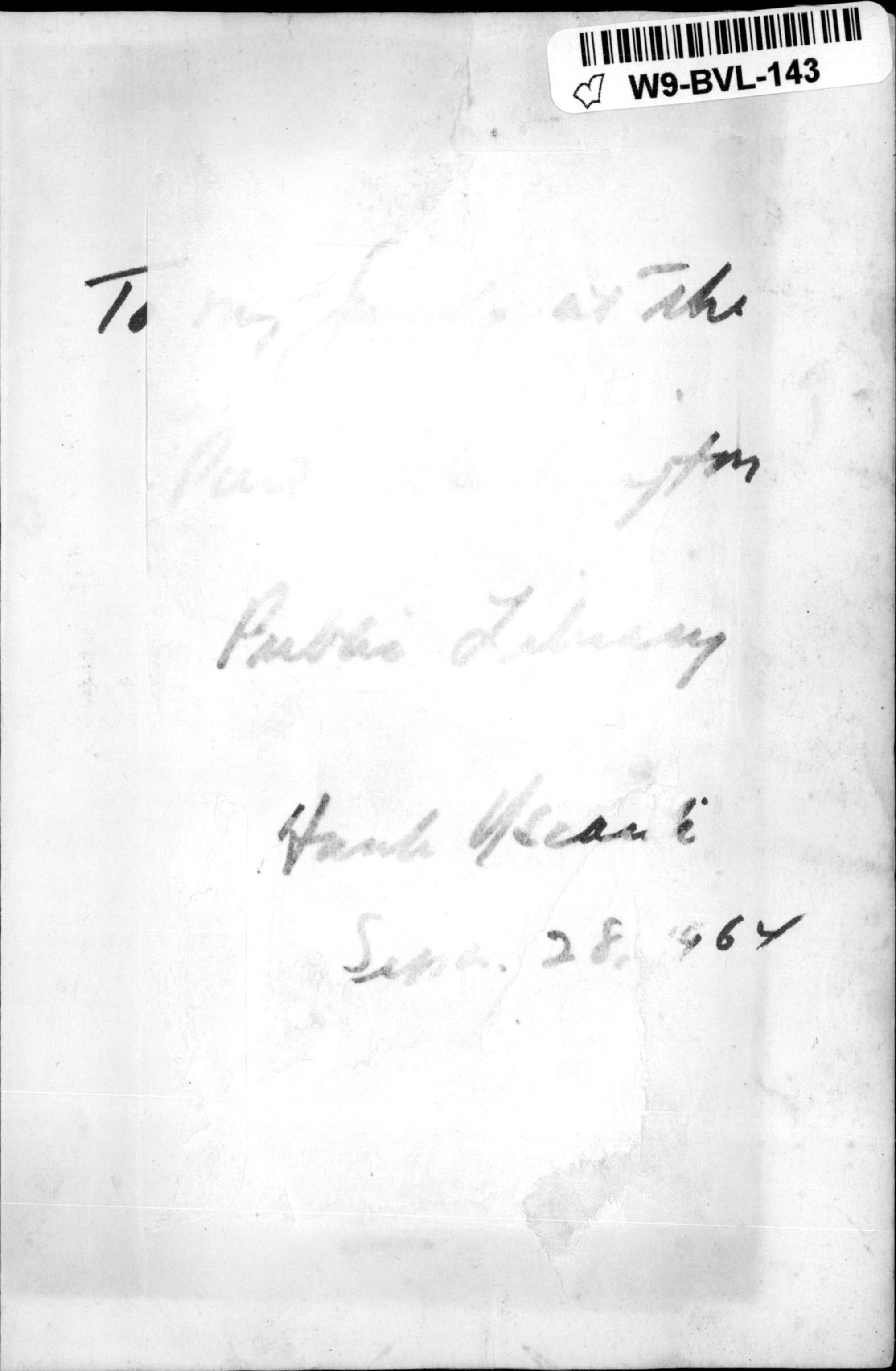
To my friends at the
Public Library
Sept. 28, 1964

A
LAUGHTER
IN THE
LONELY NIGHT

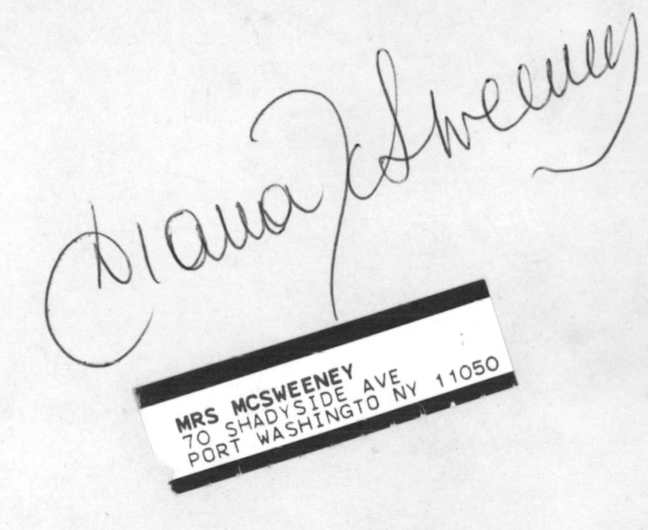

Also by Henry Viscardi, Jr.

A MAN'S STATURE: The Story of Hank Viscardi and J.O.B.

GIVE US THE TOOLS: A History of Abilities, Inc.

A LAUGHTER IN THE LONELY NIGHT

By

Henry Viscardi, Jr.

Drawings by Charles Rowe

PAUL S. ERIKSSON, INC.
NEW YORK

Published simultaneously in the Dominion of Canada by Burns & MacEachern, Toronto.

Third Printing

Typography, binding, and jacket design by Arouni

Library of Congress Catalog Card Number: 61-11433

Manufactured in the United States of America by
The Haddon Craftsmen, Inc., Scranton, Pa.

To my four angels, Nina, Donna, Lydia, and Lucia

Preface

In previous books I have told the story of my life and the story of the founding of Abilities, Inc. Now, in this book, I have achieved a purpose long cherished—to tell the exciting and moving stories of some of the wonderful people I have known.

These are the people who have gotten up one more time than they have fallen. Theirs is not only a story of courage, for it takes courage to hold fast to your ideals when you are looked upon as strange and peculiar, but it is courage with laughter and good cheer. This is always so much better, I think, than the grim kind that says it's a hard life but I'm going to do my best.

As I get older I have less patience with the pessimists, the misanthropes who speak and write of the vices and follies of man. What immense virtues he possesses! In this book I have told of the indomitable spirit and courage with which he gathers himself from the mire and plants his feet on his rough and uncertain road.

There is an undramatic quality to the courage in

the lives of these people. This is, however, what counts most, for it's most representative of your life and mine. It seems to me to be easier to be a martyr than to live every day according to one's professed principles. It should be easier to concentrate courage into one heroic act than to draw on it, just enough every day as these people, about whom I have written, have done.

Ever since I was a crippled boy I have kept a green dream growing in my heart, a dream that one day I might be the same as others, not different; that I might live and love and be loved for what I am. This is the story of other green dreams growing in the hearts of some extraordinary people seeking ordinary destinies. It is simply told as they have told it to me.

In only two instances has it been deemed necessary to change the names and identities of people I have written about—Gale and Phil.

For those whose tears and laughter are included in this story, as well as for myself, I could never singly thank the many who have helped to keep the green dream growing and helped to make it come true. May their green dreams be ever growing in their hearts and one day may they, too, come true.

Henry Viscardi, Jr.

TABLE OF CONTENTS

A LAUGHTER IN THE LONELY NIGHT

Hank Viscardi

1. Somebody in the Shadows

The dawn comes soft and gentle. As I climb out of my car, the plant looms ahead, a low elongated silhouette against the flat Long Island landscape. The hush in the early morning haze is almost oppressive. The only noise is the tread of my footsteps on the cement path.

Inside, after I hang up my coat behind the door, I walk down to the chapel, through the main office and the medical department and the conference room. The desks in the main office, empty now, are to me more than desks, just as the work benches in the production areas beyond are more than work benches and production lines. To me each one is an individual, a challenge, an impossibility.

The walls of the tiny chapel are plain red brick and the decoration is simple, for all faiths worship here—

Catholic, Protestant, and Jew. At one end there is a simple altar; at the other, carved wooden brackets which hold, at different times, statues of the saints, candelabra, or flowers. There are no pews, only chairs, and they are kept to a minimum so that there will be space accessible for those in wheelchairs. At the left as you face the altar a stained-glass window filters the early light through its deep blues and greens and amber.

That morning I knelt in prayer, alone at the altar. It is difficult for me to kneel and at night, when I listen to the prayers of my four girls, I sit on the edge of the bed.

Not being able to kneel regularly is something I miss deeply. But it is almost impossible for me to kneel in groups. I can pull myself up—with great difficulty—only by clinging to the altar rail. But when I am alone in the chapel, as I was that morning, I kneel. I pray to God for His grace and strength and help, and I pray for perspective and humility. I know that nobody is humble who starts prating about humility, and I don't talk about it. But I pray for it. I pray, too, as I did that day, not to forget that this job in our plant is still a struggle that has hardly begun. I pray for strength and guidance in directing the destinies of this plant and the more than four hundred other human beings who work there.

This book is the story of these people. These are their own stories as they told them to me. It is time that the world hears these words, I feel,—the too-long muted stories of the misunderstanding, the prejudice and foolishness and superstition, that have been their lot—

the overprotection on one side, the almost unbelievable lack of interest on the other.

I have told the stories here because I believe that, unvarnished with the superficialities of appeals, removed from the aura of the tin cup, they should be unfolded.

These are not the stories of cripples, of amputees, of the blind and the halt. They are the stories of people exactly like you, with all the deep surging impulses and all the hungry churning needs that are the birthright of every man and woman.

I was born without legs, with legs that were only stumps, and I spent the first six years of my life in a hospital, where I was operated on more times than I can remember. At seven I came to live with my family in one of the roughest areas of New York, and as I walked the streets—at seven and eight—on those padded stumps of mine, the kids yelled after me, "Hey, Shorty—hey Ape Man. Listen, Ape Man. . . ."

We were poor, my family. We lived in what was called a railroad flat in a tenement, and though we were never really hungry, we counted every penny. My mother was Neapolitan; my father came from the hills of Sicily. His given name was Onofrio, soon Americanized into Henry.

My father died when I was young and I remember him only as a strange man. Indeed all his family was strange, tied to the Old World, to old ideas, folklore and superstition. And clannish.

At the head of the clan was my grandmother, Nona, a matriarchal tyrant who ruled with an iron hand that was dipped in witchcraft. A mystic out of the Sicilian countryside, I remember her as a mysterious, dark little woman who dressed always in black, smelled of the snuff she used continuously, and held séances at the drop of a hat.

Under her thumb she held two sons by two or three marriages, daughters-in-law, nieces, and nephews. She ruled their lives with fear and incantations, with fainting spells and tears and dizzy spells, and by calling back the dead. She knew all the tricks, and she used them. I was not exposed to most of them, but she haunted my youth, and still haunts my memory of that time.

The clan gathered on Sundays and it seemed to me they talked endlessly, never in English. Not being Sicilian, my mother, although she was expected to attend, didn't "belong." As a result, she was the butt of their jokes and prejudices.

I had four sisters, one older than I, the others younger. All were born perfectly formed. There was no record of congenital deformity in the family. But when I was born, my lower limbs simply had not formed correctly and fully. My stumps crossed at the abdomen; in fact, in my infancy they could be opened up but they would spring back again. That was the kind of infant I was. Today we know that some genes went the wrong way, though we still don't know why.

When I was still an infant, my mother has told me, she went through a period when she was told, "You will have to strap this baby onto a board." My father shaped a breadboard so that there was a place for the twisted limbs, and she'd straighten them out and bind them to the board with pieces of cloth. This was not very pleasant for the infant, me, and she said I cried a great deal, which is understandable.

A few months later, my father, who was a barber, learned through one of his customers of the Hospital for Deformities and Joint Diseases. My family got me admitted as a charity patient and so my hospital life began. It was really the first life I remember and it seemed to go on endlessly. A series of operations to straighten my misshapen limbs, what there was of them, was begun and continued for several years.

What should have been legs were only half formed, like a half-finished house, you might say. There is some semblance of a knee on one and a partially formed foot and three nodules of toes on the other. Rather amazingly, there's no fibula on either limb, only tibia. Anthropologists now say that man will probably be born without fibula thousands, or perhaps millions, of years from now. I'm just a little ahead of the fashions of tomorrow.

The years in the hospital were years of pain. The life I moved out into—the life on stumps on the city streets—was almost worse. You don't grow up in the city; you survive. You learn to fight, legs or no legs, stumps or no stumps. I guess if I ever checked back on the people who lived on our block, I'd find a large percentage of them wound up in penal institutions, or perhaps even murdered or executed.

I remember the first day I went to school. I was wearing some kind of extremely uncomfortable orthopedic boots and when I ran around on these cloddy contraptions that covered the stumps, I was just what those kids needed. They pushed me around and belted me and cut me up, and before they were through they got me into an alley and took my pants off to see if I really was like everybody else.

You began to resent. Not what you were, not even that you were different from everybody else, but what they did. On your own block you made friends and protectors after a while, and no one would harm you if you were with them, but you couldn't walk down a strange street without being the object not only of curiosity but also of abuse. Kids would walk after you and hoot and holler and call you names. Adults would stand and stare, even laugh, at this funny little boy walking around on stumps instead of legs. Adults and kids would yell at you. "Hey—Shorty! Hey—Ape Man!"

The words would ring in your seven-year-old mind. At night in your bed in the dark you would hear them: Ape Man. You were a monster, your mind would say. A seven-year-old Ape Man in his bed at night.

And yet you didn't believe it. You would live, you would survive. Beyond the tenement door in the street outside was the jungle. To exist in it, to stay alive in it, you had to be as rough and tough as the rest. No one was there to shelter you. Crippled, handicapped, blind, deaf, legless—what did it matter? You lived or died on your own.

You learned stickball and softball and marbles, but you learned other things, too. You learned to defend yourself and to fight back, and once I could get hold of them I fought hard. I learned that brooms, especially the handles, could be used for more than sweeping floors, that a rock was a wonderful thing to have in your pocket or doubled up in your fist if you got into a brawl, and what you could do when you lifted your little stump up to kick a fellow in the groin. And I learned your tormenter would leave you alone, after that.

Outside, you had no insulation, no protection. Once a cop broke up a crap game I was watching. All the other kids ran but I couldn't get away fast enough. The cop picked up the pot and stuffed the coins in his pocket.

"Well," he said, looking at me as if I were probably the most miserable specimen on earth, "you couldn't run like the others."

"I wasn't playing," I said. "So it don't matter. I was looking on."

"Listen," he said, "you think I believe that, you lying little ——. If I ever catch you again, I'll break this stick over your can."

I felt it wasn't fair. I would have played, if I could have run as fast as the others, but since it was obvious I couldn't run, I felt I was perfectly secure watching the game but not playing.

But I wasn't, as I found out.

Still, even there on the street, there were other moments, other ways out of this jungle existence, other moments in the dark. I hadn't yet begun to ask myself about grown-up things—whether one day I would find a girl who would love me, or marry me, whether I would have a family of my own. The dream then was in the childhood moment, in terms of the streets and sports.

If you asked every man what he thinks of, lying in bed just before he goes to sleep, I wonder how great a variety of answers you would have. Some men must think about their work, some about music and dancing, and some about women, some perhaps of faith, and some about the bills that must be paid. I used to dream —as a kid—that I was a pitcher for a big-league baseball team, and that I was still crippled. I used to go to sleep dreaming that I was pitching for the New York Yankees and that the Blessed Mother had endowed me with the miraculous power to pitch nine straight innings of strikeouts for one entire season, every time I went to the mound.

How long ago that seemed, and how far different the prayer, from what was in my heart that early morning in the chapel at the plant in Albertson, on Long Island. We pray in different terms, at different hours. There were so many things the boy could not know or foresee —the long torturous route out of the tenement, out of despair, out of defeat, the long road to that moment in the chapel.

The long road from myself to the world, from myself to the others. The boy did not know that these others existed; to himself he was the only "different" one in all the world. We learn slowly, whatever our abilities or disabilities, and it was a long road before the boy became a man, or learned to reach out beyond himself to the others.

It was of these others that I thought and prayed that morning. Ellen, the personality girl, in her wheelchair . . . Ellen, who still, after all these years, calls me "Mr. Viscardi." . . . Peter, who walks straight and tall and full of his young strong dreams, though a few years back he could not even stand. . . . Alex, the handless, legless supervisor in the packaging department. Process packaging is one of our specialties and some of the jobs to be done are extremely delicate, and complex and difficult, hands or no hands, but Alex can do them all better than any of his staff . . . a girl who leapt through a window . . . and a boy who almost died on an island ten thousand miles away. Our galaxy of humanity swarmed into my thoughts.

Alone in the morning, questions tumbled into my mind, into my meditations. What did I understand of God's plan for me? How had I come to this place? Where was the future—and why? For all the crippled of the world, as I told myself? To show the world what we really are? Today, in effect, we are no different; we have feelings that run as deep as yours, we can laugh like you, even without hands and arms and legs; we have abilities; we have dreams; we love as you love; and we also can laugh.

Their story is my story, as mine is theirs. Their pain, their dreams, their yesterdays and their tomorrows, are mine, as mine are theirs.

Leaving the chapel that morning, I came into the warehouse area, where the ceiling is higher and there are racks on both sides, filled with steel and aluminum parts, prefabricated side sections of airplanes, packaging material, wood to be made into crates, cardboard to be fabricated into boxes, paper for stuffing or insulating material, rubberized hair or matting for packing delicate instruments. Alex's section.

Oddly, as I walked through this section I had a sense

of anticipation. The place was still half lost in shadows and interlacing shafts of light. I saw one or two foremen in the distance. Sometimes, early in the morning like this, I drop into the cafeteria for a cup of coffee and a chance to chat with the other early arrivals.

Conversations fall into patterns, like habits. They repeat themselves, and yet there is often a warmth and meaning in the very repetitions of concern.

"How's the baby, Bill?"

"Great, Hank. She cut her first tooth. She likes to ride in the wheelchair with me. Mother puts her in Daddy's wheelchair—and away we go."

"Watch out when she gets a little older—she'll drive you right into the wall."

"I got to watch out now. . . ."

We sit around the table in the cafeteria, four or five of us, in these minutes before the workday begins, and sip coffee and munch on crullers.

Often, for me, the coffee hour includes a problem that someone calls me aside to discuss. This morning, it is a worker whose child is emotionally disturbed. We talk of what to do and my advice finally is that she should make a courageous effort to have the boy committed for treatment where he can get the best care. But she is afraid to let him go, and I doubt in my heart that she will do this. She will think it over, she tells me, as she wheels away to her job inside the plant.

Cars drive up outside, bringing the workers. One of the rules of the plant is that everyone must get to work under his or her own power. Many need cars with specially added mechanisms—like Alex, for example—so that, handless or legless or paralyzed, they can still get there. We have no way of going to get them, and no one to send.

"Say, Alex bowled 147 last night. The highest score of anybody over there. They gave him a cup and they took his picture for the local paper. Say, was he set up!"

"And I hear they had a ball afterward."

"Did you say ball or brawl, Hank? What I hear, it was something hot, after the bowling. One of the fellows got home with a broken crutch."

"What happened? He fall down a flight of stairs?"

"Who knows? Just, they say, the crutch was broken when he got home and his wife was sore as hell."

"Funny as a busted crutch," somebody said.

Probably it wasn't very funny, but everybody laughed. There are questions about work . . . problems . . . decisions to be made.

"I may be held up a little today," I say. "A delegation from Argentina is dropping in."

"How many is that this year?"

"Ten countries, I think. Or eleven. But these visiting delegates do us a lot of good. They can spread the word —all over the world. Some of those places, they still think a cripple ought to be thrown over a cliff at birth. . . ."

"One day, maybe they'll wake up."

"Maybe."

"You've got to beat the prejudices, that's all. Beat 'em into a pulp."

"Sure. Sure as hell."

I listened to this crossfire a little longer and then started back to my own office. It was still shadowy in the building; most of the lights still had to be turned on. There was still the preworkday hush before machinery and people and production moved into top gear.

At the door to my office I stopped. By my desk, in a splash of sunlight that spotlighted her beauty, was Ellen. Ellen of the brown eyes and the radiance and the wheelchair. Her eyes were bright with excitement. She had, she said, something to tell me.

Ellen was one of the first to come to Abilities, in the very earliest days, when we were only getting started in a garage in West Hempstead. She has all the faults and all the virtues and all the vagaries of her wonderful Irish ancestry. She loves life and laughter and fun. She has big dreams and far reaches of imagination, and just the slightest touch of the fey. When first she worked for us, she threw herself into every individual problem in the plant, almost wearing herself out with worry over how this one would do, or how we could solve a home problem for the next. Every applicant was a personal challenge to Ellen—and many of them she helped through to victory.

But the day she came to be interviewed by me for a job at Abilities she was selling herself and doing a whale of a job of it.

She was well-dressed and attractive and alert, and she had none of the downcast quality about her that you find in many disabled people; they tell you how desperately they need a job, that they're willing to do anything—but they don't really believe you're going to hire them, and they won't really believe it until you say, "All right, you're going to work."

Not Ellen. She had something within her, a belief

that you recognized instantly. She was going to get a job. Behind the bright words and the bright smile, Ellen didn't question it for one instant. I remember thinking to myself in that first interview, as I saw this tall, charming girl, with her bright, undaunted blue eyes, "This girl can be an asset if she believes in us and isn't too cocky."

I remember I sat her down and explained to her that this wasn't just a job but also a dedication, and that some of the greatest hurts I've had in life came from the very disabled people I wanted most to help. "Some of them," I said, "have really belted me, from time to time."

Ellen looked startled. "What are you trying to spell out, Mr. Viscardi? What has this to do with me?"

So I began to tell her some of my plans, where I wanted Abilities to go, not merely as a business, but as an education in the triumph of the human spirit, as a pilot plant for all the world to copy, as a research and teaching center. "If you want a challenge like this, then we want you here," I told her. "But if all you want is a job, I don't want you to come in. You're not just routine material; you either have to be on the first team or you don't belong. And the first team is dedicated not only to the job but to tomorrow and the day after. . . ."

If I had known her then, as I do now, after our years together, I would have known how she would fill up emotionally at what I was saying, and what it would mean to her to have the chance for this kind of opportunity.

For this was the beginning. I started with a very attractive and self-assured young lady who was to become one of the most dedicated—and effective—spokesmen for the basic philosophy and meaning of this company we have built together.

So this morning, when I found her waiting in my office, Ellen and I talked. She was here for a very important reason, she said. And she told me what it was.

I do not want to tell that reason now. I would rather wait until Ellen and the others have told their own stories, because only then can the full impact of Ellen's decision and the courage it took to make it, be understood.

And so—to begin—let Ellen tell her story as she told it to me.

2. ELLEN: *A Fire in Her Eyes*

I was thirteen years old, and I was going to junior high in New York. That afternoon I took off from school and with my older sister Mary—she was fifteen—rode downtown on the subway. It was the first time we'd been on the train all by ourselves and I was pretty excited. I was always sick on anything that moved but that time I wasn't sick at all.

It was a Friday and all the way down on the train I remember Mary talking about what we were going to do. We were going to have lunch with our mother at Woolworth's and that was a big treat, a real deal. I had it all figured out. I was going to have a banana malted and a tuna fish sandwich. And I was going to get a new pair of shoes, too.

We met my mother at Macy's and did our shopping but when we went into Woolworth's to have lunch I felt suddenly ill, and I never got a chance to have the banana malted and the tuna fish sandwich. I'd never been sick like that before—or since, for that matter. I had such terrible, terrible pains that we didn't stop for anything, we went right home. The worst pains were in my legs but it was well past the polio season so no one thought about that, at first. I was very athletic then. I played all kinds of games and I was wonderful at softball—one of the stars on the team—so mother thought I had one of the charley horses I was always getting, only a worse one than usual.

The pain got worse and worse that night and the next day, and when my mother got home from work she went down and got a doctor who lived just a little way from us. He wasn't the family doctor, in fact, we'd never had him before, but he knew what it was, I guess, before he ever came up. All he did when he came in—I remember it very clearly—was just raise my head. Up till then all the pain I had was in my legs, but when he raised my head, terrible pains began shooting down my back, obliterating everything else.

Then I was going to the hospital. He sent me to the best, all right. Nobody knew how we were going to pay for it, but it was the Neurological Institute at the New York Medical Center.

You know, I felt sorriest for my parents. It was all so sudden. Mother had come home just as always that night, sure that I'd be O.K. But when I got up to go to the bathroom, my legs gave way under me and I crashed down to the floor, smashing into the side of the dresser with a wallop that must have sounded as if the house was coming down.

That was when she got really scared—called the doctor. When he came in I was in my mother and father's bed—that was a big treat to me—and afterwards he and they went out into the other room and he told them I had polio. My mother must have collapsed. Anyway I heard this terrible racket out there but I was all alone in the bedroom and didn't know what was going on.

Then my father came back—he always took over in a crisis—and told me that I had to go to the hospital. That didn't bother me. I only wanted to make sure that I wouldn't be there long. I was captain of the softball team and we were playing a rival school and I didn't want to miss that, but as long as he assured me I wouldn't be in too long, I was good-natured about it.

We lived on the fifth floor of a walk-up house, and when the ambulance came it was quite a hassle to get me downstairs and into it. They couldn't get the stretcher up to the bedroom and I couldn't walk over to it, and finally they had to carry me out.

I remember the doctor's telling my mother to burn the tongue depressor that he had used, their covering my face with a towel. I thought they did it because it was cold outside but I know now it was because they were afraid I had polio and it's contagious.

As we went down those five flights of stairs, all the neighbors were watching, and the ambulance was quite a thing and I felt like a real celebrity. Daddy came down with me and rode with me to the Neurological Center.

There they put me in a private room, and told me what they thought I had. I had heard about infantile paralysis before, because two cousins of mine had it, but the word poliomyelitis wasn't so well known as it is now and I remember thinking that one of the doctors said I had polio margarine.

They still weren't sure because I didn't have a lot of the usual symptoms. I didn't feel sick. I didn't have the high fever or the chills. The only thing was that my legs wouldn't move and I did have pains which I kept describing as big charley horses. But within two days both my legs and both my arms were paralyzed.

Then something else must have hit. I had to be fed, of course, and I couldn't keep down anything I ate. Sulfa was new then, and I developed an allergy to it. I was very sick from that, I think worse than from the polio. I developed terrible spasms that got so bad one night that I actually landed on the floor. I was so sick that at one point I had the last rites.

For nine weeks, I don't think I ate a meal that I didn't lose. I don't know—the doctors didn't know—what it was from. They gave me X-rays and everything they could think of and could find nothing wrong with me, nothing beyond the polio. I guess I had a subconscious awareness by this time that I would never walk again. I didn't tell myself, I didn't let myself think it actually, I just sort of knew that I wouldn't be able to use my legs again. But I still didn't say to myself, "Oh, my God, this blow life has dealt me." Maybe you don't, at thirteen.

While I was in the hospital, my parents and sister could visit me three times a week. I could hear the elevator and I knew it was time. Mother was always the first one off. She never walked, she always ran to my room, stopping only when she came to my door. You know, it was funny. I had always known my sister was her favorite. I sort of tagged along. But I didn't mind because Mary was always good about it and, besides, I knew that I was my father's sunshine—that's how he put it. But in the hospital, it was always my mother who came first.

After nine weeks I was sent home. I had gone down from about a hundred and fifteen pounds to fifty and I went home in an ambulance. It was Christmas Eve.

When I was carried in, the Christmas tree was up and the men carrying the stretcher put it down so I could see the tree before they took me into the bedroom. I felt pretty much like a celebrity again. Next day there were the presents, and the first meal my mother cooked for me when I was home. It was chicken and it was the first thing that stayed on my stomach in two months, so I guess I was more homesick than anything else.

I guess I knew something was happening that would change my whole life. That wonderful priest—the one who had given me the last rites in the hospital—I told him that I wanted to go into a convent, even if I never walked again. He explained that you don't become a nun because of something you've lost, you do it because everything you have doesn't mean anything and this is the only thing you want.

I had lots of things on my mind then, but the big thing in everybody else's mind was Warm Springs. The doctors at Medical Center had told my mother to try to get me to Warm Springs, Georgia, where I could get special treatment. This was during the war years, and my father was making good money in war work, but the Medical Center had been terribly expensive. We had no kind of hospitalization or anything then and we never had too much money.

My father worked and my mother, and after school my sister worked also, gluing wires and leaves onto artificial flowers and plants to make five dollars extra a week. She would bring the stuff home, too, and I would glue with her in the evenings. Everything cost money, including a physical therapist, and my parents were still paying off the bills at Medical Center, but some way we made it.

I went down to Warm Springs in August, and I stayed there a little more than four months, while I was fitted with braces. Funny, I came home on Christmas Eve that time, too. Now I was walking on those braces and I came home alone. I don't know what my family expected, but I don't think they expected to see me on braces and crutches. I could feel their shock. For just one second I was a stranger, not the girl they knew. And where was the girl they knew?

Warm Springs had a good recreational program, and good therapy. I tried another place after I got home, a sanitarium at Haverstraw, but for me it was wrong, and I came home, again in time for Christmas. On New Year's Eve we had a party and at midnight we all stood up. Crutches and braces and all, I was standing up, welcoming in the New Year.

Then I stayed at home. I was still on crutches and braces and it was hard getting up and down those five flights of stairs. The only way I could do it alone was by walking up backwards. I went to school every day and it was a matter of waiting until six o'clock for my dad to come home and carry me up the five flights—which I usually did—or going up backwards on my own. I did it when I had to, but it was a terrible physical strain.

Of course funny things—crazy things—are always happening to me. I was just home from Warm Springs, it was all I could do to walk up the stairs backwards. One day I had to go to the Hospital for Special Surgery for a checkup, and we took the subway. After we got off the train I started up the double flight of stairs one step at a time, holding onto the banister with one hand, and hopping up backward on one crutch, while my mother followed, carrying the other crutch.

It was hard and it was slow and it was tiring. But I had made it all the way to the top when a man came along. Thinking I was going down because I was facing that way, without a word he lifted me up, put me over his shoulder and carried me all the way down to the platform. There he set me down and without a word hurried off to catch his train. He didn't give me time to thank him for what he meant as a great act of kindness and he never knew I had to start all over, up those two flights of stairs.

By this time I knew I wasn't going to walk again, ever, like other people, but this didn't stop me from living or wanting to live. I had gone through grammar school and high school when we moved to a two-family house in Woodhaven, Long Island, where I had only one flight of stairs instead of five to get up. I forced myself to use the back stairs though, because they were twisting and harder for me to manipulate.

I didn't especially want to do office work but I knew

I had to do something so I enrolled at a business school in Jamaica. I'd go by myself on the bus. I enjoyed it. It gave me a feeling of independence to get around by myself. Then I got my first job, a temporary one with the Queensboro TB and Health Association. After that I'd been out of work only a few weeks when I happened to see a GIRL WANTED sign in a window when I got off the bus one day. I walked in on my crutches and I got the job. It was with a real-estate and insurance firm and not just typing and clerical work. Crutches or not, I did most of the work in the office for four years.

Then my sister Mary got married and she and Jack went out to California to live. That changed everything at home, for she and I had always had an awful lot of fun together. Mary was like a foil for me. She knew how to get the most out of me and would egg me on to do all kinds of things. When time for my vacation came around I took a trip out to California, by plane, to see her. I had a dual purpose. I wanted to see her because I missed her. And I had to talk something out with her. I had been thinking again, as I had just after I was sick, that I wanted to join a convent. I had not told my mother about this for, religious as my family was, I knew she wouldn't like the idea. But I'd written Mary about it, and she'd suggested I come out so we could talk it over.

We talked and talked and Mary thought that I should try to get a new job. She figured that was the answer to my ideas about the convent. But it wasn't. After I got back I made inquiries at several convents—the Grey Sisters of Mercy was one—but none of them I wrote to wanted anyone who was disabled. The work is too demanding, they insisted.

So I put the idea to one side. Maybe, after all, my mother was right, and Mary was right. Perhaps there was marriage in my future. I was running from loneliness, but I didn't know which way.

Maybe that contributed to my unrest after I went back to work. I wasn't happy, but I was working hard and I asked for a raise. "The job isn't worth a raise," my boss said. "You're getting $45 a week now. That's all you need, anyway. And besides, a person like you, no matter how good you are around here, is lucky to have a job at all."

Funny thing—that very night, in a newspaper, I read about J.O.B., Just One Break. It was for people who had some kind of handicap or disability, the item said, and it was to help them get jobs. Mrs. Roosevelt was one of the people behind it. And Dr. Howard Rusk.

As I read this piece I thought, "Well, this could be for me, too."

I was pretty tight for time because in the summer my boss came in only two days a week and I took care of the office the rest of the time, but I did call J.O.B. and made a date.

By then I had my own car. My wonderful family had given it to me as a Christmas present. I remember that Christmas morning I woke up and there was a little toy red car on the vanity beside the bed. I picked it up and held it and suddenly—I knew. They meant they were giving me a new real car. It was a Ford and red and beautiful and I started driving it two weeks later, when we got the hand controls installed. Soon after that I got my license.

So on my lunch hour I drove in to the J.O.B. office at Bellevue. The man who interviewed me was English and he talked on and on. I wondered if I was auditioning for him, or he was auditioning for me. Then he got up and went inside and I heard him say, "And she's very attractive, besides."

And I thought to myself, "Oh, boy, what am I getting into?"

But the next day my mother and I went out to the plant in West Hempstead that had been opened just a short time before. I knew what this new thing called Abilities was but I didn't know how I would make out. "You know," I said to mother as I was finding a place in the parking lot, "you know, I've never been much with disabled people."

I don't want to sound cold or anything, but I'd refused a job in New York City with an organization that worked with disabled people because they all looked so sad, as if they could never laugh, at themselves or anybody else, so completely as if all they had left of life were the lonely night, and no laughter across the stars. Well, I didn't want that at all. I wanted laughter and love and wonder. I didn't see any reason why I had no right to these things, just because I wore braces on my legs. I didn't want to live my life as an object of pity.

I didn't want to be with sad-looking people, people who looked and acted crippled inside as well as out. That was what I was afraid of when I pulled into the parking lot at Abilities, and got my first view of the building, an old garage that sure didn't look very imposing. But when I walked inside it was different. It was happy. There was Florence, your secretary, and she was smiling, and Arthur in the wheelchair, and you were there behind the roll-top desk.

Looking at you was different, too, Mr. Viscardi. If I didn't know you didn't have legs, I couldn't have known it. There was nothing lugubrious or anything like that in your manner. You can tell when people are happy, when there is that inner happiness, some spirit that is exciting and unexplainable but just as real as hot soup on a winter night, and you were like that, and this garage with its workers and its wires and its banging. You said all right, go to work, just like that, and Arthur was saying outside to me afterward, "What do you do and you'd better type because that's what we need and how." Well there was also some personnel work to do, too, I found out.

When I went back to that real-estate office and told my boss I was going to take another job in two weeks, he just wouldn't believe me. He kept right on acting as though it wasn't a fact. The man must have imagined this was just my way of trying to get a raise, and that no one would really give me a job except him. Finally, on the Friday afternoon when I said good-bye, he was the most surprised person in the whole hemisphere.

He said, "Ellen, don't kid any more. This is just a bluff and you know it."

And all I could say, as I packed up my stuff and got ready to leave, was, "It's no bluff. I've been telling you to get yourself a replacement. You're going to need her bad Monday morning."

So I came to work in that drafty garage and soon I was not only typing but was interviewing people myself as the jobs increased in number. And I was part of the team.

Out at Abilities, my life took on a new dimension.

It wasn't just working with you and all the others. There was a lot to learn and a lot to do. In personnel, I was suddenly on the front lines. Here they came, the lame and the blind and the frightened and the unemployable, and at first each one of them wasn't just his own problem, somehow he was also mine.

The ordeal of listening to their stories, the repetition of despair in so many, the refusal of others to quit, the certainty of others that they would make it—those interviews racked me to pieces. Two things began to be clear in my mind. One was the lack of understanding that the public has about anyone with any disability. It isn't just we who must adjust, who must understand, but the public—the man behind the desk who does the hiring, the fellow across the aisle in the subway.

But the other side I saw, too—the cripples who wanted to be cripples. A girl comes in with one arm, and she wants all the pity in the world, she wants nothing but sympathy. She's helpless. She's a woman and she's a cripple and everybody owes her a living.

"Dear God," I thought, looking at one of these. "I'm so sorry for her. But don't let me ever be like her because then I would hate myself."

You had to turn them down. You had to listen and you knew all they were saying was true, but so many had the wrong approach, the wrong things in their emotional patterns, and we wouldn't be able to help them at all, and they wouldn't be able to help the others.

My family had bought a house in Franklin Square and we were living there, but most of my life revolved around my work. I had got engaged to one of the men in the plant but my mother disapproved and—well, finally, I broke the engagement. I know now that it was the best thing for both of us, but it was an unhappy time for me. Disabled or not, on crutches or not, we live our lives with laughter, and disappointments, economic problems, family arguments; wearing braces on your legs, or having no legs at all, doesn't change any of the rest. Disappointment—and broken romances—happen to all of us.

Of course, I was still driving my car, but now I had an accident and smashed it up. Then my boy friend loaned me his and I had a slight accident with that, too. Neither was really my fault but maybe right at that time I was a little accident prone.

Then one night the real accident happened. Dad was in the garden and mother wasn't home yet from Abraham and Straus, the department store where she worked. Things hadn't gone smoothly in the office that day, nothing special, just a crumby day. But I'd usually go in to Brooklyn to pick up mother and we'd go to a novena together. When I came out of the house to get into my car it was still light and though I couldn't see him, I knew Dad was way out at the back of our lot, watering the flowers. As I went down the steps to the car, suddenly I went down.

All of a sudden my leg gave way under me. My left leg was straight out, because, with the brace on, it wouldn't bend. And I was wedged against the wall, half leaning on that stretched-out leg with my other leg useless under me.

I didn't know what had happened, but I knew I needed help.

I called out to Dad, and when I realized he was too far away to hear me, some way—I don't know how—I got up the steps and to the phone, and called the nurse at Abilities, Marguerite.

My father came in just then and I told him to go get my mother because she would be worried. Then I asked Marguerite to come over. I wasn't too upset. I thought my hip was dislocated, but that as soon as I got to a hospital they would push a few things here and there and everything would be hunky-dory.

When Marguerite arrived, the pain was beginning to set in. I'd called a doctor she suggested and he said for me to get to a hospital. But I was supposed to go for a helicopter ride the next day and I was all excited about that. Marguerite said I ought to call you, Mr. Viscardi, and I did. We talked about Parsons Hospital and you insisted I go in an ambulance. I didn't think I was hurt that badly. But then—maybe it was the state of shock or something—the thought of an ambulance suddenly appealed to me. After all my years in and out of ambulances, suddenly it sounded like fun.

So the ambulance came and we went down to Parsons and I'll never forget seeing you there waiting by the front door. My mother was there, too, when they took me down and X-rayed the hip and said it was fractured. I guess I hadn't learned much since I was thirteen and wanted to get out of the hospital for my big softball game, because when you and Dr. Marks told me my hip was broken and it meant an operation, I kept asking if the operation could be postponed a day or two because the next day I was going for a helicopter ride!

Naturally, I didn't get that ride. I stayed in the hospital and I had more operations. Oh, how you get to wondering about operations, about pain. You get to asking why. You get to thinking, oh, God, why me? I want to dance and it's polio. I want to play softball and it's bed for weeks, for months. I want to ride in a helicopter and it's a broken hip and operations and more pain. Why me, you think, and your self-pity wells up in you like a great tide and you weep with sorrow for yourself.

But that self-pity is worse than any of the rest. It is the real destroyer, because you can't fight back, you can't win back, with that consuming you. That's what cripples you, more than anything. I knew it all too well, and, except for some of those rough moments, I fought against that kind of pity, that kind of weeping, with all my strength.

The trouble was that nothing was doing any good. The first two operations to pin my hip took place over a six months' period, and I was in terrible pain most of the time, and in and out of hospitals. Summer was gone and autumn and it was getting on toward Christmas. Mary and her husband were back East and I was staying with them. She knew the pain I was in but I didn't tell mother or Dad because I didn't want to upset them right at Christmastime.

But you know, Mr. Viscardi, the day you called me into your office and you told me about the MacMurray osteotomy, that was something! They take a mallet and chisel and break the hip bone into little pieces and they put you in a cast and that way the blood goes through all those little pieces that are broken, like a hundred little islands, and the healing begins.

So I said yes, I would go through with this, but all the time something was telling me not to, that I wouldn't make it if I tried. I had just met a young man and we had fallen in love, although then I didn't realize it, but I wanted to be with him. Probably because subconsciously I knew and wanted to be with him, that operation frightened me. I kept putting it off, first for three weeks, then for three weeks more, with different excuses.

But the time came when I ran out of excuses. And I was sure—just absolutely sure—that I would not survive that operation. I never even bothered to worry about what it would be like when I came out of that operation, or what condition I would be in. I was just concerned about dying. I wasn't too shook up about it, but I figured, oh, this is the end of me. What a way to go!

I always made Communion on the first Friday of every month, and one of the promises made to St. Margaret Mary by the Sacred Heart was that anyone who makes first Fridays will never die except in a state of grace. So I purposely did not go to the sacraments before I went to the hospital that last time. In fact, the night before I went in, Frank and I went to a party. It was a terrific party. Bob and Dot and Marion and Bill, all from Abilities, were there, and by twelve o'clock we were none of us feeling any pain. My father wouldn't be up after twelve to help carry me into the house, but the others said they could do it, though there wasn't an able-bodied man or woman in the whole crew.

When we got home about three in the morning, all gay as dawn itself, they started trying to get me up the outside stairs. They were holding onto the chair for dear life but when they got to the top they realized they'd forgotten to open the screen door and they had to carry me down the stairs and start all over. Well, when they got me up the second time who opened the door but my father and mother, both something less than pleased with all this.

As I said, none of us was in very good shape. All my mother could think of was that I was going into the hospital the next day for a serious operation. I'm sure she thought I should have acted with more decorum. She looked at me very reproachfully, I thought.

The truth is, if you're going to have a couple of drinks, it's much better to be in a wheelchair than walking on crutches, because you stagger in any case on crutches, and if you have a few drinks and then try, you are really in trouble. In a wheelchair you can get away with it a good deal easier.

But I do remember my mother looking at me in the wheelchair and saying, "Have you been drinking, Ellen?"

And I looked up, hardly able to keep my two eyes open, and said, "Who, me?"

Mother and Dad didn't say a word and I just hoped I could find my way to bed.

That was the prologue to my trip to the hospital that morning. But still, I thought, I'm not in a state of grace. I haven't had the sacraments for a month, and the promise is that I can't die except in a state of grace. I really held onto that in my mind. I thought: At least I have that shot in the dark. I'm going to survive this, maybe.

It was on Sunday that I went back to Parsons Hospital in Queens. And at eight o'clock that night the telephone operator called me. "There's a priest here to see you," she said. "Would you like to see him?"

Well, I thought, this is it. The good Lord wants me to have those sacraments before I go. It was like sticking a pin in my balloon of hope. Now I was sure I was going to die.

But I didn't. And what a shock I got when I woke up! My entire body was encased in a plaster cast—from my feet all the way to my neck. For four months I lay there.

Four months of not moving is a kind of living hell, too. But there was one night when it was different. Audrey was getting married and they were giving a party afterwards. And the crowd at Abilities sneaked me out of the hospital, plaster cast and all, to go to that wedding party. They had to get a litter for me, and they had to get the doctor's permission, and they had to get a truck—a carry-all—that was big enough to take the litter without shaking me up too much, and they came up, some of the boys from Abilities, with Frank and Wes doing the heavy work, and they carried me out to the wedding party.

It was a wonderful wedding party, the way I remember it. It was all bubbles and blossoms and laughter. I really didn't have very much to feel gay about, but I was a little gay that night and talking to everybody, and I know the story was going around the party that Ellen was happily plastered in plaster. In a funny way, it was a wonderful night on the town, with Frank and all the others. And I kept wondering, even in that bubbly haze, if ever the day would come when it could happen to me. Something wonderful and real and forever, so there would be no more of the long lonely hours, the long lonely nights.

Even in the plaster cast, the dream was there. It was Frank I loved. There was a bond between us because we both had disabilities; because we were of a kind. But there were terrible problems also, terrible problems, because Frank had been married before but it had worked out badly and there was his little boy whom we all had to think of in terms of love and security.

One day, I thought, all this will happen to me, and I will be a bride . . . one day, in the bubbles of the party.

You remember things, Mr. Viscardi. After that MacMurray operation I remember a night—I think it was only a day or so after the operation itself—when you came to see me. I was in this semiprivate room, and you sat there, and I was drifting back and forth in the haze of medicines and being doped up. I was more not there than I was there, I feel sure, but I can recall looking at you once, sitting quietly beside my bed, and you were crying. I don't remember too much about our conversation or anything, but I can remember you very, very well.

Then, the time came when they took me out of the cast. I knew I'd be in a wheelchair most of the time after that. I still had dreams but they seemed far off, and meanwhile there was my work at Abilities, a job to do for others, and in that I was sure I could lose myself.

But the night the cast came off I was not nearly as

elated as I should have been. The room, the world, were suddenly different. The cast had been a kind of psychological shell of safety and now I was out of it again. I called my mother and Mary to tell them I was out of the cast, to tell them I would be going home tomorrow.

Then I called you, Mr. Viscardi. And half an hour later you were there, with three splits of champagne, to celebrate. And as we lifted our glasses to celebrate you told me that the future was going to be altogether different from the past, altogether wonderful.

But I know there was a purpose for what happened. Not just a physical purpose, I think, not just mending a broken hip. Something happened to me in that hospital—oh, I wish I could find the words to describe it. It changed my entire life. It changed my outlook. Perhaps you might say it showed me new vistas—in that loneliness I talked of, in the big questions for which, at first, I could see no answers.

There was so much I still wanted, so many wonderful things in the store window of life. There was so much to do, so much to contribute, so much that was needed in the work that we were doing, you were doing, Mr. Viscardi, at Abilities.

I remember wonderful Dr. Yanover, the Abilities doctor, coming to see me, when I was still in that cast, and sitting on the side of my bed. I was complaining terribly, nothing was pleasing me, and he grew very quiet as he leaned over and said, "Don't you know, Ellen, without a Good Friday there could never be an Easter morning?"

I want never to forget those words.

3. Moment

This was the girl who was waiting for me in my office, to tell me of her recent decision.

For each of us there is the moment—the moment of self-belief, of finding one's way, of at last standing tall and straight. To Ellen it came in the long, lonely hours.

In my own life that moment came, in a dramatic instant, with a pair of artificial limbs.

I was still very young, just out of Fordham, which I had to leave in my senior year. I took all kinds of odd jobs. I even cleaned up a fight arena—the floors and seats and the ring itself—and ran the hat concession, all on my stumps.

But I still stood a little more than three feet high. I couldn't reach the telephone in a phone booth and I couldn't hold a strap in a subway. I was a little guy hanging onto the side. Perhaps, in the deepest sense, I felt this spiritually as well as physically. The dream—the vision, the ambition, the goal and the drive—were all within me. But what was the magic to make them come true?

I worked in a law office and studied law at night, and later I got a job in the tax department of the Home Owners' Loan Corporation.

My family was living in Elmhurst, Long Island, and I was with them. I was twenty-five years old, and my stumps had been deteriorating for four or five years. The pain of them was with me all the time. I didn't know what to do. Ordinary artificial limbs wouldn't work on what I called my legs.

Out there in Elmhurst was a doctor I had known, a

sort of Viscardi family physician since we first moved there from Manhattan. A big, warm human being. I met Dr. Robert Yanover again when my mother had some surgery done, and I told him about my legs. "Come back when you get your mother all straightened out," he told me. "We may be able to do something about it."

When he examined me later he told me, "If you don't do something about limbs you'll spend the rest of your life in a wheelchair. You want that?"

So we started making the rounds, trying to find someone to make me a pair of limbs. A lot of experts said it couldn't be done. My set of malformed stumps simply presented too many problems of balance and weight pressure for any ordinary set of artificial limbs. And the prosthetic art in those days—before World War II—was not nearly as advanced as it is today. At that time, anybody could be a legmaker. You beat the thing together out of old tin cans and pieces of wood and leather and you were in.

Dr. Yanover kept hunting for the one for me, and finally found him on Third Avenue, under the Elevated that has since been torn down. He was a remarkable old German, a craftsman of the old school. But in those 1930 years of propaganda that deceived many people, even in America, the old German did not take graciously to Dr. Yanover, a Jew. He told Yanover, "I don't want you in this case from now on, do you understand?"

Outside, I told Yanover to forget it, I didn't want this man, we'd find somebody else. But Yanover said, "No. What do I care what he thinks about me? I only want to help you get limbs, Hank. And—whatever else

—he is one of the best limbmakers in the city. He is the one I want you to have."

It is no easy job, and there are endless fittings, but finally the day comes. Suddenly, I'm standing up. I don't even have long pants to cover the limbs when I first look at myself in the mirror, and the old German lends me a pair of his to see what I look like, but he is a short, pear-shaped little man and the pants are too baggy in the seat and too narrow at the ankles, and I look like something out of a comic strip. But I'm standing there and I see the man that I might have been years before. It was an overwhelming experience. I know there were tears coming down my cheeks.

He said, "You'll walk."

I said, "It's so painful. I can't, not now, not tonight."

And he said, "You'll walk."

He was a tough old Prussian, a militarist. But he broke out a bottle of beer, some beer that he got in his Yorkville bistro, and we poured the beer and drank a toast to the future.

I was deeply grateful to him, and to the training over weeks that was to enable me to walk like any man on those limbs. But that night as we drank our toast, I also secretly toasted the man who had led me to this shop and who later became the medical adviser of Abilities—Robert R. Yanover, M.D.

That was it, the whole moment of transition. The world in that instant was changed for me. I could stand up in the subway, walk down the street, see the tops of cars, and go dancing with lovely young ladies. My world changed, my world began.

The war came and I joined the Red Cross and

worked with the disabled. I did rehabilitation work in the service hospitals. After the war, I worked for the Mutual Network as assistant director of special events and sports. Eventually I joined Burlington Mills as personnel director.

I was interested in small boats and I lived on a houseboat in Long Island Sound from where I drove to work with no difficulty at all. And I met a lovely girl who had her limbs and was beautiful and a good cook besides. We were married, and, on a plot of land at King's Point, next door to my friend Dr. Yanover, we started to build our home, much of it with our own two hands.

But the great dream, the vision within, does not quickly or easily die. Mrs. Eleanor Roosevelt and Dr. Howard Rusk and others were urging me to come back to rehabilitation. I was needed. There was a post to be filled as head of an organization they called J.O.B.—Just One Break. Located in a small office in New York's Bellevue Hospital, it paid little in comparison to what I was getting. Its future was, at best, obscure. Its purpose: to find jobs for the disabled people nobody wanted to take a chance on.

I didn't need it. I had it made already. I was no longer Hank Viscardi, the legless wonder. I was Mr. Viscardi, head of personnel for Burlington Mills and a rising figure in the industry. There was no practical reason to give all this up, to go back into the world of the disabled, as the head of J.O.B.

But in the final analysis this was the course that seemed to offer the greatest challenge.

And out of that job came in a few years, the new venture. In a garage in West Hempstead, Long Island, we started a new nonprofit business nobody but a handful of us believed in—Abilities, Inc.

It has become something of a legend now—how the first four employees had, in total. five good arms and one good leg.

We added other workers as our first jobs began to come in from plants in the area. We were operating on a strictly business basis, competing against bids of other electronics firms. We were promising the highest quality workmanship. And some of the big plants were willing to give our new operation a chance.

Soon we had thirty employees crowded into that West Hempstead garage. It was cold, drafty, improvised, and wonderful.

To this place were to come the army of the disabled, some of them looking for work, some for sympathy, some of them ready to work, some of them too lost, too helpless, ever to work. Some of them exciting and dynamic.

Peter was one of these.

When I first saw Peter, he could not stand at all, or walk, except with the most uncontrolled muscular movements, spastic and jerking and seemingly insane. His huge frame would sway back crazily, or plunge forward until his long arms would reach out to the earth to halt his fall.

Ellen, head of personnel, saw him first. She came to me and told me about him, his strange uncontrolled body and arm movements that seemed to preclude the possibility of a job of any kind, and yet she also told me, "He wants to work, Mr. Viscardi. Oh, how he wants to work."

The job application blank I had designed had certain questions that were supposed to give me clues to potentialities. One of these was a series of questions about hobbies. If a potential employee is disabled, as all of our employees are, I wanted to see how, in his spare time, he developed recreational abilities to overcome disabilities. Strictly on his own.

Peter's application blank listed undeı hobbies: A lathe and a drill press that he ran in the cellar of his home. Machine tools—run by a youth like this, who, according to Ellen, had no control whatever over these muscular spastic movements of arms or legs or shoulders. Certainly this in itself was a sign of initiative, courage, plain old-fashioned guts. I read on for details. He was not machining metals, but wood. With all this obvious disability, he was running a wood-turning lathe and operating a drill press.

The thought came to me as I read the application that here was a clue. What was happening to him in that basement shop was what happened to many cerebral-palsy people. He was almost completely controlled when doing a particular job operation. That was all I had to go on. That—and the fact that Ellen told me, "I never saw anyone who seems to want to work as much as this boy."

So I told her, "Ellen, from all the facts, my impression is that it may not work out. But what can we lose? Let's give it a try. Tell him I want to see him."

And Ellen had wheeled out of the office to bring in Peter that first day.

To begin with, he was unable to sit in his wheelchair without falling out of it, because of the convulsive movements of his pelvic region. But within weeks he was performing—brilliantly—a very demanding job. To see him operating an armature-winding machine while he hooked one arm over the back of his chair was unbelievable. But this he did.

Many months later, he and I sat down together in our office and he poured out his story.

4. PETER: *A Tall Young Man*

I remember one of the first jobs I ever got in my life. I was just out of high school, right at the start of the Korean War, and I used to work in Red Hook, Brooklyn, way downtown near the docks. I worked for the Police Athletic League, sort of checking in people, and I got a dollar a day. It was a job for me, that was all. At this time I used to walk, well, like a snake.

Talk about handouts! When I came home, half crawling out of the subway, people who didn't know me used to hand me money. They made me feel like a Bowery bum, and they made me mad. One time a big fat lady told me she had hit on a horse at the race track that day and she handed me money and I threw it on the ground and she came back and picked it up and walked away.

I was traveling three hours a day from my house to that part of Brooklyn, working for PAL—they work with the youth gangs—and I was getting one dollar a day, but my mother always said, "At least, Pete, you're getting out. You're doing something."

My first day on that job was pure hell. The people acted as if they thought I came out of the zoo. It's a tough neighborhood and I walked six blocks from Carroll Street to the police precinct where the Athletic League is. I couldn't walk a block but I made myself do it. After the first day it wasn't so bad. That gang—they were real tough kids the public were trying to help—used to walk me to the subway nights so nobody would bother me, and a longshoreman used to take me home from the subway by car after he got to know me.

My father's a C.P.A. and financial adviser for a big company and we have a house in Flushing where we live and where I grew up. I guess I was just an average kid till I was about ten and this thing started. It came gradually, so I didn't really notice it at first. When I was about seven my toes curled a little. Sometimes a curb would be higher than another and I'd fall. That was all.

Then, when I was ten, in grammar school, my right arm began to curl out when I wrote. So what did I do? I changed off and wrote with my left. My aunt always said I had used my left hand when I was a baby so I wrote with it, but I always threw a ball, a football or baseball, with my right. I had played games up till then but I had to quit after my right hand seemed to retract whenever I tried to grab something.

My family didn't know what was wrong and I went to an orthopedic doctor. He said I had hammer toes so I had plates put in my shoes. They didn't help either.

My toes dug into the plates and it hurt a lot, so I tried to invent ways of my own of walking.

Things happen you can't control. One time, when we were going to the orthopedic doctor downtown, a horrible thing happened. It was no one's fault. My mother looked at me and I'll never forget the look on her face. It was panic, almost. She seemed worried. "Peter, look at yourself." I had never really looked at myself before in my life. I mean, I was never vain. I was only thirteen and at that age you're not vain, I guess. I'll never forget this thing. I looked at myself in the showroom window. There I was walking like a pregnant lady with my stomach out.

It was the first time the thing had hit me in the trunk of my body. I couldn't hold it still. Every time I tried to hold it in, it went out with a jerking motion.

Well, it kept getting worse, this thing, this jerking thing in my body. One day that winter, when there was a foot of snow all over the ground, this thing hit bad and seemed to be bounding all over the place. I had to get home and it was five blocks. I used to have an English racing bike; I could always ride it, even when I couldn't walk. I started through the park and then I fell off the bike into the snow. I was still about two blocks from home, so I picked up the bike and carried it and I crawled through the snow like that.

A boy with me saw all this and said, "Peter, what's wrong with you?"

"I don't know," I told him. "I can't walk."

I was jerking, my whole body was jerking, all the time I was crawling like that. I fell with my face in the snow and I lifted it up. The boy wanted to help me to my feet and I said no, I couldn't stand.

Then a tremendous spasm hit me and I was bent almost double, but I kept going, crawling fast, plowing through the snow, like a bulldozer.

Then I got to the stoop of my house. My grandmother was there. I was her pet and she was all upset and excited when she saw me. She asked me, "What's wrong with you? Get up on your feet. What are you doing, crawling like that?"

I didn't know what to say, so I just went upstairs and I went to bed. In the middle of the day I went to bed. When I was sleeping, I was perfectly normal, like anyone else.

That was just a little while before Christmas and it was one of the first bad Christmases I remember. My family called a doctor, but he couldn't tell what was wrong, so he just said I must be tired and for my parents to put me to bed. After that my parents had the best doctors and when they just couldn't afford the fees they had me go to clinics. At first some of the doctors thought it was cerebral palsy but all the tests showed I didn't have that and what they told my mother was: "We don't know what is the matter with him. We just don't know."

When it first began, the family doctor, he's a wonderful man, suggested a brace to keep my toes from curling back. The brace was real expensive, $110 dollars, but the pain got so bad that I used to take it off during school and put it on when I got home. Of course that caused trouble with my mother who said, "Now you've got something to help you and you take it off."

But I thought to myself, "Gee, I can't stand the damn thing."

Finally, I threw it away. I couldn't use it. Another $110 shot down the drain.

I wasn't old enough to appreciate it then, but I realize now that, through everything, my father, who paid the brunt of it all, never said a word. He was always in there trying to help me. Both he and my mother always did everything they could for me. The doctors themselves didn't know at that time what was wrong with me. They were trying to help me, too.

For me it was plain hell all the time. Even my family didn't know what ailed me. When I had to go to the bathroom, I wouldn't tell them or anybody; I would roll up the hall, into the bathroom, pull myself up, do what I had to, and then roll back and pull myself into bed.

Then my parents heard of a famous doctor who had developed a special nerve-block operation and who once even spoke before Congress about it. They took me to him. At that time, if I used every ounce of energy in my body, I could walk in a cramped position—duck walk, I call it.

Well, they took me to him. He gave me a twenty-four-hour physical—the works. He looked me over. He sent me to other doctors. He had me X-rayed. He sent me to a place where they took all kinds of specimens from me. It cost my parents an awful lot of money. Then he called my mother and father to his office and said to them, "I can cure your son."

My father said, "You can cure him?"

"Yes," he said.

My mother asked him, "One hundred per cent?"

He said, "I can cure your son one hundred per cent but it would have to be done in the country. I have a summer place near here, in the country."

My parents were a great deal upset at this. I could hardly walk and I couldn't even dress myself. But the doctor said, "Why can't he come to the country? I'll take care of him."

So they talked and he convinced my parents he could do it, and I remember my father's telling my cousin, who used to help me get dressed, "We're going to send him to the country. He's going up there and get well."

So we all went, my mother and father with me. My mother was going to stay with me, and my father shortly afterward went back to the city to work. It was midwinter and cold but they were doing the best for me that anybody could do, my parents were.

We stayed at an inn. Then the doctor got busy. He gave me vitamin shots. They didn't have tranquilizers then, and what he used to do was to hypnotize me—or try to—and keep my muscles going with some kind of muscle reactor.

He had a chart with circles on it and he would use it to hypnotize me. He never could put me under, as he called it, but I did get drowsy and my muscles would relax a little. For a while he was doing it every day. He said the cause of my trouble was that the pituitary gland secreted too much fluid because I had grown too tall too fast. His treatment seemed to help some because I did seem to relax and I could stand. I could put my right foot forward all right but when I put my left foot forward my body arched backwards. I couldn't walk.

It was costing too much at the inn so the doctor said we could stay at his farm. My mother and I moved over there and my father went back to the city to be with my sister. We didn't pay anything at the farmhouse but my mother helped with the housework. She thought she was getting her boy cured and she'd do anything for that. And I did seem to be getting better, a little. I know now that what was happening—the seeming improvement for a time—was just part of the pattern of my real trouble, that they didn't know.

We were there for six months and it cost my parents $1,600. My father had to borrow to pay the doctor, who insisted on the money right on the barrelhead or he couldn't go on handling me. And they were so sure he was doing me good, they got it up.

By that time this doctor really liked me and wanted me to stay there. But after six months my mother said to me that she wanted to go home, she had to, and she told my father, "I can't stay on and I don't want Peter staying."

Well, the doctor came into New York. He always stayed at a hotel in the middle of the city and he had me go there for treatments, all that hypnosis business. My mother asked me about what he did and I told her.

"Does he really hypnotize you?" she asked.

I said, "No, Mother. I just get drowsy like I did up there."

She said, "Well, it costs $90 every time you go there and get drowsy."

The next time he got me to the hotel and started to give me the old hypnotism again, I kept my eyes open. He talked to me and I looked at him. He looked me right in the eyes and he had hypnotic eyes. He looked into you, you know, and now I looked right back.

He said, "Don't you feel a little drowsy?"

I said, "No."

He put down the card and said, "Don't you like me any more? I'm a friend of yours. We used to talk when we rode around in the car together in the country."

I said, "Yes, I like to ride in the car and all that but I never knew this was costing my parents $90 every time. They can't afford money like that." He didn't say anything so I went on. "Do you realize how much money my parents have put into me, even before I started coming to you, more than half a year ago?"

He didn't say anything. So I said, "Aren't you going to cure me?"

Still nothing. I said, "I'm starting high school now. Bayside High School. I want to be like the rest of the kids. When am I going to be cured, really cured?"

He didn't say anything; he just walked out of the room.

While I started putting on my clothes, my mother was getting ready to pay him. I said, "Don't pay, don't pay him, Ma, he didn't hypnotize me."

That started a terrible argument between them. Later he wrote a letter to my parents saying he had cured me as much as I could be cured. He couldn't do any more, he said, because I had what he called "hysteria."

Well, I stayed better and I didn't shake any more and I went to high school. When I put my left foot forward everybody laughed, but I kept on in school for three years. Then, in my senior year—I was seventeen

—I began getting worse again. Still nobody knew what was wrong with me, and my mother was worried about this hysteria thing. She sort of wondered, I guess, was her son nuts. She took me to a family doctor who had taken care of her when she was a child and who had seen me before.

He was a pretty elderly man. He looked at me and said, "Well, you sit up straight. You don't jerk any more."

"No, I don't."

"Why is that?" he asked.

I looked at him and asked, "Can you tell me, Doctor?"

He said, "We're going to send you to a new hospital."

This new place was like a country club. It was for people who had money. Actors and actresses went there. People with nervous breakdowns. High-class alcoholics, who went there to get what they call "dried out."

The thing I had—that they didn't know—affects you in different ways. In the morning when you wake up, you're almost perfect, and you can walk to the bathroom with no trouble. That lasts only a little while, but it's why my mother got to believe that it was hysteria and only in my mind. She would see me in the morning and she'd say, "Son, if you can walk like that in the morning, why can't you walk like that all the time?"

She wasn't sure. Was I making it up, putting it on? Was it all in my mind? We didn't understand, you see. Nobody did. And she had every reason to believe this doctor who said I did it just to make an exhibition of myself.

So I went to this hospital and I stayed there a year, to be cured of all this hysteria I didn't have.

During my time there I saw people I'll probably never see again. I saw people from the concert stage, violinists and other musicians, who had had breakdowns. And I can tell you one thing—in that hospital you saw people at their rawest.

But they took good care of me. I was going around happy-go-lucky again. There I was away from home and on my own and everyone treated me like a king.

I took some school courses, and even picked myself up a girl friend, a nice girl, a little high-school kid who'd had a nervous breakdown. I saw quite a bit of her. I used to ask myself sometimes what she saw in me, a big gawky guy who couldn't walk right. Just the same we were together a lot and she would cry a lot. Then the doctors sent her home, saying that she shouldn't have been there, that there was nothing the matter with her.

They were still puzzled about me. There would be conferences and they would discuss my case and they'd go through all their Freudian theories and rip apart my mother and father, trying to find out if they didn't want a child when I was born, and on and on like that. I mean the stuff you used to hear in those conferences was enough to turn your stomach.

Of course I was embarrassed about being there because all the time I just didn't think I was nuts. That's why I didn't want my family to come to see me, because I was embarrassed.

But they came just the same, and sometimes I'd go home for weekends. By then everyone seemed to have the idea that I had what is called "conversion hysteria." I'd converted my hysteria into these symptoms. Funny —of everybody, my old grandmother was the only one who knew. "I'm telling you there's nothing wrong with his mind, nothing at all," she cried out once to my parents and some cousins when I was home for the weekend. "There's something wrong with him physically. We have to find the answer to that."

My mother would say, "Pete, if you had something like polio, if you were in a wheelchair, if you couldn't walk, it would be different. Pete, are they right? Maybe you're doing it in your mind . . . ."

And there I was, six feet and taller, and still walking like a gawky child.

When I got home from the fancy sanitarium I wanted to go to work. Mother thought it would be good and asked the doctor. Then I said to her, "I'm going to pay you back, Mom, as soon as I get a job. All the money, all the thousands and thousands of dollars you've spent on me, you and Dad."

My mother said to me, "Son, you don't have to do that."

I said, "I'm going out and get a job."

Well, I tried, but nobody would hire me. People used to laugh and say to me, "You want a job? Why don't you just go home and watch TV?"

So after a while I went home and watched TV and one day my mother asked me, "Why don't you go to work? And if you can't work, why don't you go to school? Do something, Pete. Something. Anything."

The doctor, you see, had told my parents that my "illness" was all put on. He told them not even to drive me any place, to make me walk wherever I wanted to go, because if they drove me, psychologically I'd figure that I was getting what I wanted, and I was using this way, this jerking of the body, as a tool to be domineering or some bull like that.

But I managed. I had a friend drive me to Jamaica and I went to the last year of high at night. As usual, I passed all the courses and I was graduated. Whatever else, I got that diploma.

That was when I went to work for the Police Athletic League, for a dollar a day.

Going back and forth, I used to meet a lot of people. I love to talk to people and I'd always tell them different stories about what was wrong with me, though never that some people thought I was crazy. I'd say I'd been in the Korean War . . . or shot in the back . . . or I was a motorcycle rider who'd got bounced off his cycle.

Some people don't care or understand, but some are wonderful. Like one subway motorman who got to know me. The stairs at the station where I got on came down in the middle of the platform—and some of those Brooklyn subway platforms are almost a mile long. The train stopped way down at one end and I'd have to walk all that way, with everybody on the platform looking at me as if I were a drunken bum. It was hell. But that motorman used to stop the train where the stairs came down so I wouldn't have to walk. I was like the king of the subway there.

My next job was at R.C.A., right near my home, as a telephone solicitor. I got $23 a week, which seemed like big money, but everybody else, all the fellows my age, were coming back from war, and getting jobs in factories or going on to college. I was lonely. I wanted to work in a factory. And I kept thinking to myself, how do I get in a factory, how do I get a job? I tried a few. I'd wait for hours, sometimes all day, and then they'd say, you look fine, but the way you walk—a lot of people don't like to see cripples. I got so that when I heard the word "cripple" I just wanted to hit somebody.

I still had my job at R.C.A. and I still had the psychiatrist to pay—I was going for treatments. All the money I made went to him and finally I just decided I was through. I had no life, no social life, no friends, no future, no hope, no happiness, no nothing. I decided I'd just sit home there in Flushing and watch that damned TV and watch it and watch it until finally I would go crazy, just like they all thought I was.

Then there was a change at R.C.A. and I got laid off. I went down to the Unemployment office and they took one look at me and said, "Fellow, you couldn't get a job anywhere, anyway, so we'll mail your unemployment check as long as you have it coming. Just go home and stay home. *Don't waste your time looking for a job.*"

My best friend was a neighbor kid. His mother used to say what a shame it was that I was home all the time, and I'd make up stories about working but of course she knew better. Berny and I had grown up together and when we were in high school I protected him because I was always big, and he was small. His mother used to say, "There's a handicapped boy protecting my Berny."

Berny and I used to go swimming. I always liked that because in the water I could walk almost like anybody else. One day another fellow with us asked me why I didn't try a place called Abilities. "They take handicapped people," he said.

"Maybe I will," I answered. But I was thinking: Why should I go all the way out there just for someone to say no to me? And I forgot about it.

But Berny remembered. "Gee, you got to try something," he told me. "You're always in there fighting, trying hard. When are you going to get yourself a job—and work? This place hires handicapped people."

I says, "Yeah." But inside, I start telling myself, handicapped people, sure, but not like me.

My friend Berny says, "Listen, we'll drive you out there, me and Eddie."

So they drove me out to the first Abilities plant. It was in the winter of 1952, when your plant was that garage in West Hempstead, long before this big new one with four hundred people.

I went in and I saw Ellen. She made me sign some papers and asked a lot of questions, about my hobby and all, and I told her about my machine shop and how I fooled around with wood carving. She asked me if I wanted to make out an application, and told me to put down all the stuff about my hobbies.

One of the men who interviewed me that day was a fellow named Fred. I had to walk through part of the shop to get to his office and I thought all those people would be looking at me and laughing the way they did other places when I went to get a job. I remember I saw one fellow sitting at a desk. He was one of the top executives, and he was in a wheelchair. He smiled at me and I said, oh, gee, the first person who ever smiled at me in a factory.

I noticed everyone was busy working at a bench. Some people were in wheelchairs and some were—I mean, had legs off. I noticed all this maybe because though I was handicapped, I'd never been in contact with handicapped people. When I got to Fred, first thing he said was that I had a pretty good handwriting on my application form. I wondered why, but I learned later he had lost his right arm in World War II and had to teach himself to write with the left.

I told him I'd been at R.C.A. for a year and that now I wasn't doing anything. He said, "Do you think you'd have any trouble getting here?" That's what he said—"trouble getting here." My God, did I have a job, I thought?

I said, "Oh, no. I don't care if I have to crawl, I'll get here."

"Well, you live in Flushing. That's pretty far away," he said.

"I'll get here."

I couldn't wait to tell my folks that I had a chance to work at this place. But my mother was working then, in a beauty parlor, and Dad was at his office and my sister was in school. There was no one at home to tell. Then the phone rang and who was it but that Ellen.

She says, "Can you come to work Monday?"

Well, that was Friday night. Monday! When she says that, I say, "Sure, I can come to work Monday."

Boy, was I happy! I'll never forget that moment. I was almost crying.

Then my mother came home.

"I've got a job," I told her.

"You've got what?"

"I got a job."

I told her, and my father and sister came home and I told them, and my mother called my grandmother to tell her, "He got a job—Peter got a job. Yes, I know it's hard to get there on your own." Abilities was running no bus trips for the handicapped. You got to work on your own, and you did a day's work for a day's pay. That was it. No handouts. No charity.

To get there was rough. From my house, first you had to take a bus to get down to the main street. Then another bus to Jamaica, and from there a Long Island bus to West Hempstead. But me, I didn't care. I was going. I had to leave very early because it was hard for me to walk. The streets were icy and when I came to a street in Jamaica the cop said to me, "You're crazy trying to cross that street. People are crawling." I should have told him I could crawl better than most people, but I just said, "I'll make it." And I crossed the street, running and slipping, but I didn't fall, and I had to wrap my nose around a telephone pole to stop. Anyway, I got out there. I got to work and I got there on time.

My first boss was Alex, in packaging. He didn't have any arms or legs. I used to watch him sometimes at work and I used to say to myself, "Gee, there's a guy like him. He's much worse than I am." It was the first time in my life I didn't feel crippled any more. I started helping other people around, doing things, picking up things that they couldn't handle. And I started to feel more normal. More normal than I had ever felt before in my whole crippled life. So I began to work in the plant and a whole new world began to open up for me. It was something I'd always believed in and yet I'd almost been ready to write it off.

Darkness at Dawn

So here I was working, and the people at Abilities didn't look at me as if I was a spook or something, and I guess I'd never been so happy in my whole damned life. I saw other things around the plant that I wanted to do, and I got transferred a couple of times, till finally I got to wind armatures, and I did it for two years. And it was the only thing that kept me going after I started getting worse again.

Good as I felt about having a job and all, I still wanted to get well, and all the money I earned at Abilities went to paying for psychiatrists and doctors, but I never told them at Abilities about that. I lived at home, but now I was paying my own medical bills, anyway.

I went to one psychiatrist for a year before he told me he couldn't help me, and then I went to another, not very far from home. He took a look at me and said, "I don't think you have conversional hysteria; I think you have some sort of neurological disease."

And you know what I answered—me, who'd been claiming all the time I wasn't nuts? I said, "Doctor, you're crazy. I've got conversional hysteria. I'm sick. Are you going to treat me?"

But he got me to go to a neurologist, who took a look at me and said, "You have dystonia."

I looked right back at him and I said, "What's that?" And then I went back to Abilities and told you, Hank, what he had said and you said, "Didn't you know it, Peter?" And it turned out you'd known about it for a long time. All the time I'd been knocking myself out going to psychiatrists—and paying them—without letting you know about it, you, Hank, had been trying to find out what was wrong with me, too. I've heard all about it since: how you talked to Dr. Sverdlik, one of Abilities' examining doctors, about me, and how he'd known right off the bat what none of all those other doctors had been able to discover with all their examinations and X-rays and stuff—what was wrong with me.

Sure, it's a rare disease. I know that now. And I know it's related to Parkinson's disease and that it's what they call a "discoordination of the muscles" and that it hasn't a thing to do with emotions or conversion hysteria, or being off your rocker. But all the things that had ever happened to me—the jerking, the spasms, even the way my toes curled when I was a kid—were all signs of this dystonia, and in seven years in and out of hospitals and doctors' offices nobody before had ever tied them all together and come up with the answer.

I didn't know any of this till later, because you, Hank, didn't want to get me all excited and hopeful until you knew what could be done. You talked to Dr. Howard Rusk and from him learned that a Dr.

Irving S. Cooper had been fixing up a lot of people with Parkinson's disease with a fancy brain operation. And you wanted to know about whether such an operation would cure me before you told me about it.

And about the time, Hank, that you were ready to tell me, I got the same answer from this other doctor—and told you. But then I was in a hospital again, for another couple of weeks and another batch of examinations and tests.

There they kept giving me drugs every six hours, night and day. At first, it was tranquilizers, but they didn't help. Then they used some kind of heavy drugs and I felt like I was drunk all the time. Then they said to me, "There's an experimental operation and there's a doctor here who might want to try it." Somehow you found out about that, Hank. I don't know how, but you did. And one of the men in the office—Art—called me on the phone. "Don't have that operation now. Hank says don't do it."

"I'm going to have this thing," I told him. "I'm going to get well."

Art pleaded with me not to do it. "Come back," he said. "Come back with us. Come back to Abilities."

I insist I'm going to have the operation. I don't know what I'm saying. All the time I'm talking, I'm drunk on those pills they feed me. I can't even walk. So the chief surgeon, who's going to perform this what they call a chemopolidectomy on my brain, he comes in to see me. One thing I've sort of learned in all these years of hospitals and doctors and people telling me this and that, I've learned to take a stand and to analyze people a little. And this surgeon seemed a little nervous. First he said to me, "You're a strong boy but we have to do something for you."

I just looked, I didn't answer.

Then he said, "You can have this operation if you want it."

I said, "Doctor, you're the head surgeon here and you're telling me I can have this operation if I want it. *You tell me you want me to have it.*"

The surgeon just turned, without a word, and walked out of the room.

After he was gone, I picked up the phone and called my mother. "Come and get me," I said. "I'm coming home."

I don't know why they did it, but when I left that hospital they gave me fifty one-grain tablets of sodium amytal. It was supposed to make me feel fine all the time, so when I got home I began taking it, but what it did was make me drunk all the time. I was going around like a crazy man, staggering, uncontrolled. I did all kinds of crazy things. I told off my parents. I even got mad at my mother and hit her. I never meant to do a thing like that. I didn't know I was doing it, not really. Then my mother—the day after I did that terrible thing to her—asked me to give her those pills, and I did, and she threw them down the toilet.

And I got a little better and went back to work in the plant. But I was still sick. And one day, Hank, you and another man came by my place on the work bench—you said he was a Dr. Rusk from Bellevue Hospital. This Dr. Rusk stopped and you said to him, "Now if you think you can help this boy you'd better tell him and he'll be after me all the time. That's the way he is."

He said, "Well, we have a Dr. Cooper and what he

does is put an injection into your brain, in a certain spot, that kills a little globule there with a drop of alcohol. It's not really as simple as that but maybe he can help you."

That was all that happened. I know it took a lot of doing that I didn't know about to get to this Dr. Cooper and see if he wanted to try this operation on me. But I wanted it so much. If there was a chance that I could be like other people, could walk like other people, I wanted it, with all my heart. I'd take the chance, over and over.

Then one day I got to see Dr. Cooper. He looked me over and said, right away, "I can perform this operation and if you have it you might have a new life. It might work. What do you think about it?"

I said, "Well . . ."

And he said, "Well, you have to make up your mind."

Just like that. I said. "Wait a minute. I just don't know. *But I want it done.*"

So he said, "All right. Talk it over with Hank."

The way I felt then, I didn't care if I died from the operation. I figured I was better dead than the way I was. I loved my family, but I was grown up. I was at the end of that road—and the end of the road with myself.

Plus that, I was getting sick again, back to the way I was when I was thirteen years old, and I was getting so I could do nothing. I had no control over my movements. I was stumbling and falling, and I was thinking, "My God, I'm going to lose this job now, the only thing I have that's keeping me alive." That's how I felt.

I couldn't be operated on until December, more than

six months away, and I did not know how I could go on living until then, for every day I got worse. So I went to your office, Hank, and told you how I felt, and you got mad at me, one of the best things that ever happened to me. I'll never forget it in my whole life. "You're going to have to make it," you said, "until December. You want to quit here and stay home? Well, stay on till December, then."

But I said to myself, "Hell, I ain't gonna stay home."

Then my family called you, Hank. They all loved me, and they all realized now all I went through, but they didn't want to take the responsibility of saying, "Go ahead and operate." We all knew the risks. I might come out not remembering anything. I might be paralyzed. Nobody could tell me. It was a terrible responsibility to put on your shoulders, Hank, and I know you spent sleepless nights worrying about what might happen if I did—and what might happen to me mentally if I didn't. So there you were—and there were my parents and me, and Dr. Cooper. It's like a play on the stage. Which way do we go?

But you told my parents, "Go ahead. Let him do it."

If you were wrong, I wouldn't know the difference. But you would. And my parents would.

In December, I went into St. Barnabas Hospital in the Bronx.

That operation was something!

First off, I had a Yul Brynner haircut. Then, on the day of the operation, they wheeled me into the operating room and sat me up while someone gave me a spinal injection. They put a fist in my stomach to make the spine stick out so that they could hit the right spot —and it hurt. But I didn't care; they could have cut off my head at that point and I wouldn't have complained.

Then I got a little sedative injected into a vein so I'd keep calm and quiet during the business of the day. But just in case I got a little frisky, they put a harness on me. It had setscrews, and when they screwed them into my skull—five of them—I could feel them, all right. But when you figure a thousandth of an inch may be the difference between life and death, you're not going to complain much about a few screws.

I was lying down, now, with my head propped up, and they injected some novacain into my skull and started cutting. I could feel a little ripping and a phht! when the surgeon opened up the skin. Then he began to drill and that was the worst sensation of all. I felt as if one of those air drills Con Edison uses to dig up the streets was going right through my head. And finally came the needle. It makes a hissing sound as it goes in, and after it's in, they take an X-ray and stop the operation till it's developed and they can see how far in the needle is. Then there's more hissing while they go farther in, and they do it all over again.

They were putting a needle in there through my skull, to reach a little spot on one side, so they could inject a drop of alcohol and kill that spot inside my brain. It took an hour and a half and it seemed like two years, like forever. You have a needle in your head and you feel like you want to rip your head off, to rip off all those gadgets they have on you, and run away, but you don't because you want more than all this hell to get over being sick.

Then it's over, finally. They take you to your room. There's a tube in your head. And your parents are there. They ask you how you feel. And you tell them, "I'm fine. I'm feeling fine."

But I was still shaking. I felt happy-go-lucky and maybe a little better—but I was no better physically. The operation didn't work, that's all.

Then they explained they had not gone deep enough; they had not found the exact spot in the brain. But they said they would try again. They would go deeper. It would be the same thing, the same side—the left side.

Did I want to do it? Sure. Let them try once more, I thought. Well, I let them try it the second time. When I got in there on the table, Dr. Cooper asked me, "Are you nervous, Peter?"

I said, "Yes, I am. Boy, I'm telling you something doctor, I'm real nervous."

And because I remembered the whole thing, I described the whole operation to him.

He was surprised that I remembered it all, or realized. His coldness—it was just a cover. When you realize the terrible responsibility on his shoulders you know why he developed it. I wasn't just a person from any place, I was from Abilities, and I was there because you asked Dr. Rusk and Dr. Rusk asked him. I mean, it put a lot more pressure on him.

In all my life, when the tension is real, I don't cry, I make a joke of it. All through that second operation I was joking with Dr. Cooper's assistant and telling her

I'd like to see her with her hat off, and I'm telling her I want a date with her. Right while the needle is going into my head we're talking and joking, and she's telling me she lives in the Bronx and I'm asking her if she's single. I asked them so many questions I had them all laughing, and finally the anesthetist said to me, "Peter, you'd better be a little more quiet, because you make the surgeon nervous."

When I heard that, I clammed up fast.

And then they stopped. Dr. Cooper asked me to lift my right hand. It felt all right, a little tingly, though, and a little numb in my fingers. "How do your finger tips feel, Peter?" he asked.

I said, "Well, gee, Doctor, they feel a little numb."

"How does your leg feel?"

I said, "It feels a lot more alive than it ever felt before, but that feels a little numb, too."

He said, "That's all right, Peter. The operation worked."

Well, they had that needle in me—they kept it in for a week—and they rolled me back to my room and into bed. All night they kept waking me up and turning me from one side to the other. They'd given me a sedative, and I didn't quite know what was going on for a while.

But when I woke up it was morning. It was light. I saw the nurse. She asked me how I felt. I said I felt fine. I said I wanted to get up and walk. She said, "Oh, no. You can't get up. You have to wait a week before you can get up and walk."

So I didn't get up right away. But I sat up. I sat up and then suddenly I realized that for the first time, the first time in years, I wasn't shaking. I could sit up without jerking.

Then I started testing myself, you know, the way you do. I noticed on my left side there was a little bit of shaking, but I knew that would be there until they finally operated for that side, too. On the right side I felt calm, just like the Pacific Ocean.

Well, the whole family came to see me. Everybody. Mother and father and grandmother, uncles and aunts. My grandmother even brought me a kolbossa. That's a kind of German-Polish sausage, wonderful with sauerkraut and boiled potatoes. She was sure the hospital food wasn't good.

There were tears in my mother's eyes as I sat there on the side of my bed, with my legs over the side, not shaking, not jerking or anything. My sister cried and my father looked as if I had made a touchdown or something big.

My feeling at the moment was like a man who's climbed the highest mountain in the world. He's sitting on the top, looking down, and all the world and everyone is down below. I was sitting on the side of the bed, dangling my legs over the side, and that was my Mt. Everest, right in that room.

I hadn't walked yet, so I didn't really know the whole story. I still had that needle in my head. All bandaged, covered over. After my family had gone, I said to the nurse, "I'm going to the bathroom."

She said, "Oh, you're not allowed out of bed. Not off the bed."

So I swung my legs around and I got off the bed.

I didn't know what was going to happen. I just knew

—I prayed—I prayed to God I could walk. And I walked. I just walked away from the bed, straight and not jerking, just straight like anybody else, into that bathroom.

The nurse didn't try to stop me. She stood looking at me and when she saw me walking, she turned and ran out of the room, calling for Dr. Cooper.

He was there in the doorway when I came out of the bathroom, walking. He didn't seem surprised or anything. He just said, "That's good. You look wonderful. Don't do this too often. But you look all right."

It was something, the way he took everything in stride. I thanked him for what he had done for me. I said, "Boy, you did change my life, like you said you would."

I remember the day you came to see me. You saw me there and you said, "Can you sit up, Peter?"

I said, "Can I!"

And I sat up. You just stared. It was like something out of this world. You kept saying, "Wonderful, it's wonderful. . . ."

I said, "Hank, watch this."

And I got up and walked across the room.

It was a day or so later when my father saw me walking. I was coming out of the solarium with a wheelchair. I was using it to guide me because my left side was still a little numb from the operation. But my father saw me standing up and walking without any of that jerking or crazy leaning backwards and forwards, but walking straight like a man. "Son, you look good, you look great," he said, and I don't know which of us felt prouder.

I knew I still had one more step—the operation on the other side. It would have to wait a year at least. But already I was dreaming of my life to come.

I still had problems. We always have problems. I went out with the boys. For the first time in my life I felt like a human being and, boy, I lived it up! There I was, just like everyone else, big and tall—my parents, for the first time in about ten years, measured me, and I was six feet three. But then—I began to get worse again. The uncorrected side began to go out of control and there was involuntary shaking on that side that became more and more severe. We all knew what was happening and what it meant. I had to have that other operation.

So I went through it again, all of it, on the other side of the brain. They told me it was dangerous again, more dangerous than the first time, but I didn't care. It had to be. And it was tough. There was one time when my heart was pounding as if a man's fist was inside trying to beat its way out. I said to myself, "Oh, boy, I hope I make it." And I wasn't even thinking about walking right.

But I came through. I came through great. On both sides there was no jerking, no shaking at all—just a man tall and straight, walking, like anybody else.

5. The Bench

Symbolically, to me, the work bench represents the fulfillment of the life of a workingman, whether a Peter, an Alex, or any of the others. It is the means to the end which gives him dignity and self-sufficiency and happiness that come from self-support and from work. It is to me what the carpenter's tools were to the Lord, what the fishing fleet was to the Twelve. It's what we were created for. It's the symbolic representation of everything we strive for—not to be supported but to support ourselves; not to be different but to be the same.

The bench symbolizes all that I believe is the fulfillment of our destiny as people. In a technical sense it represents the quality of integrity that I feel should be Abilities in action.

The bench is the heart of our plant, the heart of our job. It is not one thing, actually, but many, not one individual, but many. Here in the plant, as you walk through, you see them, the maimed, the paralyzed, the chair-ridden, the palsied, the legless, the armless. All of them at different jobs on what we call the bench. Amid the burr and buzz and roar of machines and stampings, they seem no different from any other workers in the world, in their attitude and their intentness on the job. They are human beings productively at work.

Yet in each of their lives I know there is a special story, a special turning point. Like Peter, each in his way faced the bleak road of disability and the despair normally associated with it, the halfway life. And, like

Peter, each in his or her way has won a victory. Somehow and somewhere a turning point was reached.

For each of us this turning point is a life-or-death moment, although it may not be recognized at the time, a pitch of crisis that determines our destinies, our futures, our lives. For there is salvation, even from ourselves.

For me, the turning point was long ago when they made me a pair of legs and I stood ten thousand feet high. For Peter, it was that day he walked out of the bathroom, no longer a quivering, shaking grotesquerie as he had seen himself, but a man. For Ellen it came in those hours of loneliness in a hospital bed.

I walk through the plant and see their faces, and chat with this one or that, and our talk is easy banter. Most of them call me Hank. Nobody thinks of me as being apart from them. The boss and they are one.

But I remember their stories, even so. Each to me lives in his own milieu of drama, the drama he or she fought to triumph in his own terms, his own private pursuit of the freedom to live, to seek happiness, to seek to contribute.

Sometimes the struggle is against the incapacitation itself. Once, I remember, I flew out for the dedication of a rehabilitation center in a Midwestern city. The whole community turned out for the occasion. Photographers were there and reporters and town officials, to witness the laying of the cornerstone of this new center. The money had been subscribed by the citizens of the community and the Rotary and Kiwanis clubs, the housewives and church people.

All of them were proud of this building, which was

to be used for the rehabilitation of crippled children. The trowel used to put the cement on the cornerstone was handled by three individuals—the mayor, the head of the local medical society, and a wonderful little boy, an eight-year-old lad on crutches, with braces on both legs. The photographers had a field day at that cornerstone ceremony.

Afterwards there was a luncheon at the biggest hotel in town and I was the guest speaker. I did not say quite what I think they expected. After the usual witty statements a speaker is supposed to make, I told them, "And now, to get serious, I would like you to come with me in time—fifteen years from today. I don't want you to change a thing. Don't change a single thought that you have. You are no older in years; you are as you are now.

"But it is fifteen years from today and you are listening to me in this room. And then you go home to your own living room, and your only daughter, whom you dearly love, is bringing home for the first time a young man whom she wants to marry. The doorbell rings and in she comes, and who's with her, fifteen years older, but the boy who laid the cornerstone today, with a brace on each leg and a crutch under each arm, and this is the boy she wants to marry.

"What would your reaction be?" I demanded of that audience. And in the hush afterwards, I added, "Anyone can love a crippled child. It's easy. We love children anyway, and a crippled child melts the hardest heart, you know.

"But what when the crippled child becomes the crippled adult? When he goes out to get a job? When he comes to your home as the suitor for your daughter's hand? What superstitions, what prejudices, do we labor under when we look on a crippled child grown up? What would your reaction be when you realized that your dearly beloved wanted this boy for a husband and the father of her children? This is the heart of the question. This is what we have to talk about today."

It was hard, yes, and maybe cruel. But it led into the discussion of the realistic job they could do with this rehabilitation center for children who would also, one day, grow up.

But disabilities are of different kinds and degrees, and not always are they visible, or measurable. There are cases, too, where it is not society to which any blame attaches, but perhaps ourselves.

The sunlight through the windows of the plant falls on the face of a woman. She is working with wires of various colors, interlacing these wires into a portion of an assembly. It is delicate, demanding, tedious sometimes, but exciting in its ultimate purpose, for this is part of the electronic computer we make for one of the larger business-machine corporations. Her fingers move nimbly in manipulating the wires.

Others working at the bench are doing similar tasks. The woman is part of a camaraderie that all accept and understand at the bench, the comradeship of the job, of creativity itself.

This is Gale. Her story, as she told it to me, is somewhat different from the others. For it is not only a story of what life did to her, but also of what she did to herself.

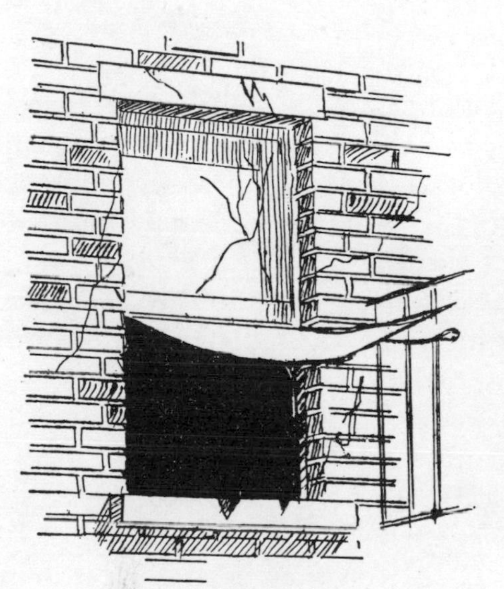

6. GALE: *The Window*

I grew up in several neighborhoods, all of them bad. When I was four years old, I was attacked by a man, in a hallway or a cellar or a yard. I don't really remember it; it is like a shadow in my life, but a shadow you can't shake away. "Something happened to her," was the way I heard it. "Something happened."

After that I was sent to live with some other people and with a woman I called Mama who wasn't my real mother at all. She took me with her when she moved to another neighborhood. There was a speakeasy below us in the place where I lived and she would go downstairs, knock on a door, and get a bottle for a quarter. There were bums in the house and drunks—and there were times when I didn't eat.

There was a mission downstairs, too. We kids all used to flock in there on Saturdays when they had services; at least we got a meal out of it. All we had to do was sing hymns.

Then I guess Mama realized she couldn't keep me. She couldn't afford to take care of me, and she was in no condition to, most of the time, so she sent me back to my real mother, who I thought was my aunt.

I was about eight or nine then and to get to my new home I had to walk what seemed like many miles to me at that age. I was a skinny, anemic kid and I was wearing an old coat and a hat pulled down over my head. I must have looked pretty odd. I knocked on the door. I said, "Mama said you should keep me."

Anyway, this woman who opened the door—my real mother—took me in, and I lived with her for several years.

She was very strict with me, overly strict. Her husband, who was really my stepfather, though I didn't know it then of course, didn't work regularly. I used to get to the movies on Saturdays and Sundays, though, even if I had to sneak in, which I usually did.

I never knew my real father. I was always told that he died in the war, but I guess I don't believe that. And I didn't get along very well with my real mother. Even after she told me she was really and truly my mother, and not my aunt, I didn't believe it, or I tried not to.

We fought a lot, especially when I was about fifteen or sixteen and wanted to go out on dates. She wouldn't let me go out with anyone except Irishmen. If the name was Irish, it was all right. It didn't matter what the individual was like; he could be a drunken bum and it was still all right. But I couldn't even go to a movie with anyone else.

At school there was an Italian boy named Buzzy who was a wonderful dancer. I loved to dance and when he asked me for a date, I said yes. But when he called my house my mother said, "She isn't home and anyway she can't go out on a date with you."

I didn't know about their conversation and when I went downstairs with the dog there he was in the vestibule. He told me what my mother had said and I said, very point blank, "Gee, I'm sorry for what she said but I can't do anything because I can't fight her. She won't let me go out with you because you're Italian."

So I didn't get to dance with him.

Then I went out with a Jewish fellow, who was a very nice, wonderful person. He came up to see me one night when there was another boy there whom my mother liked, a real fine Irish boy. When the Jewish boy knocked, my mother just told him to get lost, or words to that effect, and slammed the door in his face.

She used to get very angry with me. She'd get me down to scrub the floors and then stand over me and kick me and call me names. When she'd hit me, I'd try to strike back, and we had some terrible fights. One day she said she was going to "teach" me—with a big chain she was going to beat me with. That did it. I ran out of the house and went back to the woman I called Mama, who, I found out, in that crazy mixed-up situation, was really my aunt.

She was still drinking terribly. She would have hallucinations and imagine all kinds of things that weren't happening at all. It got to be a real nightmare and one night when she had me tied up to a dresser, I cut myself loose and ran out of the house. It was about three o'clock in the morning but I got on the subway and went back to my mother, my real mother. When I got there, about four in the morning, I went up to the roof landing, where there was a little space inside the door, and tried to go to sleep. It was terribly cold, so finally I went down and knocked at my mother's door, woke her up, and asked if I could come in. She took me in and gave me coffee.

I stayed with my mother then for a time, my mother and a younger sister who was only a kid. When I couldn't stand it any more, I ran away and went back to my aunt's.

And on a blind date I met a boy. He and I went out together a lot, and one night, when we were going to a formal evening party, he and his mother and sisters asked me to come and get dressed at their place. When I told my aunt she said, "Why don't you take your clothes with you—all your clothes—and see if they want you to stay with them all the time?"

After the dance they asked me back to their house and I told the boy's sister what my aunt had said. She told her mother, who agreed that I could stay with them if I did the cooking and cleaning and the rest of the housework.

A few months later the boy and I were married and lived with his family for a time. Then we moved to a furnished room. But we were on relief, home relief, most of the time. In a couple of years, after our little girl was born, we lived for a time in a cold-water flat and I took care of everything. It was always like that.

Then after a while, he just left. He walked out and

that was that. He walked out even before I had my second child, a little boy.

Well, I wasn't any angel. I wanted to live, to have a few moments of happiness, of peace, of joy, of feeling like a person. Sure, I went out. Why wouldn't I—why wouldn't any human being? And I fell in love with this fellow.

And sometimes, in the evenings, I'd drink, too. I don't suppose that's too odd, considering all I'd seen and heard in my life. One night I stopped in alone at a bar where I used to go and had a drink, all alone. The bartender kept filling my glass and I didn't have brains enough to go home. After a time I was so giddy that nothing seemed to matter.

It was then that two fellows came in—I knew one slightly—and they suggested we all three go to another bar, which we did. Then they suggested going to my house. That seemed all right, too, but first we went to another bar and had one or two more drinks. By that time it was about two or three o'clock in the morning, and we kept drinking all that night and all through the morning and into the next afternoon.

A lot that happened I don't remember, but I do remember the fellows saying they had no money and I told them, "Oh, for God's sake, don't worry about that, I've got money. Let's go back to my place and get some food or something."

So we all went to my place.

I don't know. Maybe I expected to see this man that I was in love with. But after I got those fellows to the house, even in the haze I was in, I asked myself why I was bringing them to my apartment. I wanted to get them out and I told them so, but they wouldn't leave. One of them went inside and lay down on the bed. I followed him, threw a glass of water over him and told him to get out. Then I went out to the kitchen and within a few minutes both of them were gone, along with all the money in my pocketbook—all the money I had in the world.

I had to do something. I went out looking for them in the neighborhood. I went down to the bar where I'd met them, got their address and went there. "You took my money, didn't you?" I said when I found them.

They denied it. "Why would we do that to you, Gale?" they asked.

Then one of them said, "If you're really broke, I'll lend you five. Will that help you?"

The way he said it made me feel cheap. "No, no, I guess you need it more than I do," I answered.

I don't remember going back to the bar. I don't remember anything. But as I found out later, I did go back, and this fellow I was in love with was there.

He'd heard about my drinking bout with the two men and he called me every foul name anybody could think of. He said I was the filthiest and the rottenest and worse—that I was no good for one single thing on this earth, not one single thing.

All this I heard later. Myself, I remember nothing of what happened in the bar. But I do remember being out on the avenue and trying to explain to him about my money. I remember his taking my pocketbook and dumping it upside down on the pavement so that I lost everything inside—my social security card, everything.

The next thing I knew I was at home, though how I

got there I don't know, and he was getting ready to walk out for good. All sorts of wild, crazy ideas were going through my head. My mother had never wanted me, I was thinking, and he didn't want me. In all my life nobody ever really wanted me.

That is the way I remember it, but it is all lost in the mix-up of despair and drinking. I can remember screaming and struggling with him. I can see dishes broken. I can hear crashing sounds. I can remember a box of letters—a whole box of love letters I had kept. You can't really store up love in a box, I suppose, but I was trying; every letter any boy or man ever wrote me saying I was nice or good or pretty, or how he felt about me, I had kept in that box. We fought over the box and he pulled the letters from me, but I had the box itself and somehow I got into the bedroom with it. I was sitting holding it and thinking what a joke it was, because nobody loved me or wanted me and now this man I loved was calling me a tramp, and walking out on me.

I couldn't stand it. I couldn't stand what I was doing to myself or what the world was doing to me. Not for one second more. I put my hand across my face, I jumped up and ran through the rooms and hurled myself right through the window. It was five stories up.

I landed across a wooden fence. It went through my back, severed nerves in my spine. One leg was hanging by a thread. But I don't remember any of that. I remember nothing. I was unconscious for about a week or maybe longer. It was a long time.

When I came to, I was in a hospital. I was told that detectives brought this fellow there, and asked me in my unconsciousness why he threw me through the window, or whether he did. I must have told them he didn't do it, because they let him go. I've never seen him since.

I spent three months in that hospital, which was run by nuns. Almost every bone in my body was broken. I couldn't even lie on the bed and one of the nuns made a special hammock thing for me out of canvas and weights and I lay on that for three months.

My children were staying with my mother.

Then I was transferred to a hospital run by the City Welfare. There wasn't any rehabilitation program then in that hospital. The patients used to joke that when you went in there you didn't come out until you came out in a box. But I fooled them; I came out after three years. Alive. Not walking, but alive. I was in a wheelchair. I had only a little money but I got myself a basement apartment and my children lived there with me. There was no way of getting my wheelchair up the stairs so I stayed in that apartment for a year without ever going outside.

I had a decubital ulcer as a result of what had happened to me and one doctor wanted me to go to another city hospital for treatment and for the rehabilitation that they were just beginning to learn something about.

After my first stay in this new hospital I could walk some, with braces, and even got up and down the steps to my basement apartment. Then I went back a second time, for a lot of surgery, and I was there a year or more. The doctors did wonderful things for me. The hole in my back, which had been like a gaping crater, was completely fixed up by means of plastic surgery, and another operation made it easier and less painful for me to walk.

I had known I was in bad shape because while I was in the first Welfare hospital I'd sneaked my medical report into the bathroom to read. A lot of it I didn't understand, but one thing I did. The report said that my decubital ulcer would never heal, and that my life expectancy was six months.

That was in 1944.

When I came out the second time, I was like a different person. I got out of the basement and into an apartment on the first floor of the same building, and I didn't want to live on home relief any more. I had found out something in all of this—how good people were. Even my mother had kept my children and had taken good care of them. I've always been grateful for this, and to other people, even some I hadn't liked, who had been kind.

In 1950, I had reached a point where I knew I had to do something for myself. Why, I probably couldn't have said. But I wanted to get off home relief, I wanted to earn money, I wanted to make my life mean something and not be just a waste. I began applying for jobs I saw advertised and I got one finally, in a factory right in the neighborhood where I was living. My daughter would push me all the way to the factory in my wheelchair before she went to school and pick me up in the late afternoon. I stayed there from March until June, but then the decubitus ulcer broke open again. I was incontinent and couldn't get to the ladies' room. As a result this infection set in and I had to go to the hospital. At the rehabilitation hospital I was told I would have to stop work because of this problem—I learned my doctor there gave me only a year to live—but I refused to quit working. I couldn't and I wouldn't—no matter what happened I couldn't bury myself forever in a room and just sit there waiting to die.

But I needed help, that much I knew, and when I was back at the hospital again, for still another operation, I heard about an organization called J.O.B.—Just One Break. That was in New York City. It was run by a man named Hank Viscardi, who got jobs for people who were incapacitated in some way. I went there, to the office in New York, and was sent out to Abilities to talk to you, Hank. One of the hospital staff drove me out. And you read all my story and you said, "You've been through a lot and you've learned a lot and you want to do something now?"

Funny. Talking to you, Hank, made a difference. Why, there were people in this Abilities place far worse off than I and they were working, and they were happy. They were in front of me, they were looking at me, and they were my friends. Right away I was sure that someone seemed to care, care deeply and really.

Of course, there were others who had. They had been doctors and nurses and people in agencies and even policemen. They had cared. All of the other side I knew well—the barrooms, the pickups, the drifting in the night, the bleak rooms, the long corridors going into nothing, the steps that go down to nowhere but hell itself probably.

But you, you and this place were something else.

I said I wanted to get a job I could hold and you said, "You've got one—as soon as you get a means of transportation."

I was staying in the city then, but, wherever I stayed, getting out to Abilities was going to be terribly difficult, and getting rides out impossible. I didn't know how I was going to do it. My first idea was to buy a car at a public auction by the city of unclaimed cars—I'd read about this in the paper—though I didn't even know how to drive. A newspaper reporter saw me in my wheelchair there and asked if I was interested in buying a car. I said I was and pointed to a big blue sedan.

"If you get the car, can I take a picture of you in it?" he asked. I said "Sure"—but I didn't get it. Two men were bidding against each other and the bid went up to $150 which was more than I could afford. But the newspaperman took my picture anyway, and wrote a story about me, a nice story, telling how I needed a car to get to work at Abilities. After it appeared on the front page of the paper, I got a lot of telegrams from people who were sympathetic, from more people, more understanding people, than I ever realized there were in the world.

The next thing, a radio program called and asked if I'd be on their program and when I got to the station, parked outside was the car and the man who had bought it at the auction. Now he was giving it to me, the radio station announced on the air.

So I had a car and I went down and learned how to drive and I got my license, wheelchair or not. After that, I went back to J.O.B. The man there wanted to send me to some place in Mount Vernon where he thought I might get a job. But I said the place I wanted to go was Abilities and that was it.

I began to work. In the first few months, I realized the whole world had changed for me. When I was in

New York, I had met a fellow and we'd fallen for each other and were married. He jumped around from job to job and disappeared once before he left me for good. That was the last I heard of him, but this time I didn't take it so hard. I had my job at Abilities and in April of 1953, months after he left, I moved out to Long Island, so I wouldn't have so far to go.

The road is long, from where I began. The past, whatever happened, is behind me. I can't change that. Then what is important? What counts for me? It is that all of this has led me, useless and impossible and unwanted as I once thought I was, into something important and good. I am a part of what you could call a wonderful pilot operation for human beings, helping in that way to help maybe hundreds, maybe thousands, by what happens in this place where I work. By what happens to me.

I can work. Science now has a way of taking care of my problems so that I can work. I'm crippled but I can drive a car and hold down a job and perform useful and important jobs in a normal routine and live, within the limitations of my disability, a normal life.

Even more important, I have found deeper meaning in my life. For the disability I had before, the disability of despair or maladjustment, of wrong and destructive thinking and attitudes within me, whatever caused them—that tore me apart a lot more than what I did to myself in that plunge to the ground.

So you see something did happen, something good. It was like beginning a new life. My son and daughter came to live with me. When she was grown, my daughter went on her own, and my son, though he had his problems like most boys, grew out of them. I have friends and I can do a lot, wheelchair or not. I can bowl. Men seem to like me and find me attractive. I get along. I have dates and parties. I live my life and work hard and feel a sense of accomplishment because my work contributes to the world and to people like ourselves, and I pay my own way.

I'm glad I made it here.

7. Package Deal

We run a business at Abilities but we deal in people, not boxes; we package dignity along with other items of merchandise. We do reconstruction jobs on people like Gale, who had been in some ways her own worst enemy. But a man like Alex, who was born behind the eight ball but refused to stay there . . . he's done as much for Abilities as we could possibly do for him.

We need some information on packaging and I switch the intercom and ask Alex, supervisor in that department, if he has a moment to stop by.

Everyone at Abilities has some special ability—and some special disability as well. Secretary or telephone operator, package room chief or vice-president in charge of manufacturing. Each has his reason for being there. But few have the time to remember in the press of getting a day's work done. This isn't a social-work theory; this is a fact of life.

So Alex comes in.

He comes in from the shop, and he's been doing some difficult business out there. His face is smudged with the marks of hard labor, his hair is mussed, and he's muttering to himself and grinning and wiping his brow with the halfway little stump that goes for an arm. Alex has no arms and no legs, just short little eight-inch stumps without hands—those are his arms—and short stumps for legs.

Because he has nothing to hold on with if he should stumble, nothing to catch his fall, it would be difficult for him to wear artificial limbs at work. So he doesn't—

anyway, he has spent a lifetime learning to live without them. Alex wore artificial limbs the day he was married, so he could stand up straight and tall beside the beautiful tall blond girl who became his wife and the mother of his two children.

I know all about that because I was best man. . . .

When I first saw Alex, I didn't tell him I was disabled. I thought he knew, for I had told him that everybody in the shop had a handicap of some sort. I had a letter about him from his cousin, and I could hardly believe that this fellow with no arms or legs could do all she said he could. But I thought, well, anything is possible and if this bird is real I want him around here.

But when he came in I looked at him and for just a minute I saw myself. I remembered when I was just his height, struggling around on the little stumps just as he was.

That's why, I guess, I subconsciously assumed he knew about me, because I knew about him. Because I remembered going to employment agencies, where I could barely peer over the tops of the tables, and getting the brushoff everywhere. I knew all this fellow must have gone through before he said "hello."

Alex was born like this. It was a thousand to one shot for him all the way. He had nothing in his favor at the start—except his indomitable determination to be something under the roughest conditions. You get to be a friend to someone and you know him, not just as a fellow worker but as a friend, close and warm and real and forever, and that is how it is with Alex and me. I know his story intimately, because his life has become a part of my own, his victories and defeats are mine as well as his. And once, long ago, he sat down in the chair across from me, and leaned back and crossed those rugged stumps of his, and began to talk.

8. ALEX: *Legless in Coney*

I was seven when my family moved from Manhattan to Coney Island. I don't even remember how early it was when I began to realize I was different; I always seemed to know, and I was always ready to fight for what I had to. Not that I wanted to fight anybody, but I knew you had to stand up and let them know. Everybody needs to be independent. If you can't be, you have to rely on somebody else and you find out—early you find out—that the person you are relying on may not be there, even if it's your own sister or father or brother, and you've got to get things for yourself, whether you've got arms and legs or not.

I was a scrapper from the time I could walk and some kid started to call me a name. So I don't have legs and arms—only short little stumps, and I don't have hands to clench into fists. But if anyone gets close enough they'll find out they've been in one hell of a fight. That was my attitude. I was taking nothing from anybody.

Back in Manhattan the kids knew me and accepted me the way I was, but when we moved out to Coney, it was different; it was rough. I was the new kid and I was crippled; I was the guy to jump on, and the name calling started, too. "Hey, Shorty!" Or more likely, "Hey, Banana Arms, lookit Banana Arms!"

Kids are curious. They want to see what you're like, how you'll react if they insult you. I was like that, too, I think. Bounce up to somebody just for the hell of it. But the first three months in Coney were a battle, I can tell you. One kid really clobbered me down a cement stairs. I was trying to protect my brother because this kid hit him and I didn't like anybody hitting my brother.

One night I just waited for him to come home. There was a little walk and a door he had to go through to get to his house and there I was, blocking the door, just waiting for him to walk in. We had a real clobbering good time there. They had to break down the door to stop us.

The time before I'd had to have four stitches but this time I came out on top; he had to have more. It was a real go-round but we were great buddies after that.

I could do something besides fight with these stumps of mine. I could handle a baseball bat with these half-size arms, clasping the end of the bat under my armpit. I could hold a bowling ball with my stumpy arms and slap it down the bowling alley. You learn to use the weapons you have, even these of mine, in the jungle of the streets. You learn to defend and to hit back. You learn to vie in competitive sport.

You learn you can win sometimes—even with almost nothing at all.

I was always a good athlete—I suppose you'd say I was a good competitor—and a good ball player. Down at Coney, the earliest ball I played was in the wide ramps that lead off the boardwalk and the people would crowd around just to watch me, because I had no hands and still I could play. That got annoying. I wasn't planning to be any freak for people to gape at.

I didn't know anything about swimming when we moved there but the kids used to play a game called torpedo. I was it—the torpedo. The kids would grab my stubby arms and legs and swing me back and forth and then—kerplunk, in I went. I don't know why I didn't drown. But I didn't. Instead, bobbing like a cork, with stumps threshing and stubby arms flailing, I could swim with the best of those guys before I got through.

It was a rough neighborhood, one of the roughest, but after a few fights, and a few experiences like playing torpedo, those kids got to know me and to know they couldn't push me around, really, and so I was one of them and it was O.K. all around.

But the authorities wouldn't let me go to school. I had what was known as home teaching. The teachers came around and I had assignments and homework. When I was about ten we got burned out of the place in Coney and moved to Flatbush. There the school was within walking distance but they wouldn't let me go. They said the classes weren't adjusted to me.

So I had home teaching all through grammar school and finally I was graduated. I went around to P.S. 181 and, along with some other kids, picked up my diploma. I don't know whether it was the whole class or not. The only ones I'd ever seen in that class before were the teachers and me. When I decided to go to high school and tried to enroll at New Utrecht High, they didn't want me either. They took one look and said, "Oh, he couldn't make it. It's too hard for him. We'll let you know" . . . all that kind of thing. But we appealed and kept appealing to everybody in the school system and finally they capitulated to all that pressure and I was in. What a fight—just to get to school! And a school that had special classes for the handicapped, besides. Well, I made it.

Getting there was a big deal. It took an hour and a half by the school bus for handicapped kids. I got up at six to get to school that started at nine. We'd get there around seven-thirty. The driver would drop us off and go to pick up a lot of other kids for grammar school. So we had about an hour and a half with nothing to do and you know what a lot of kids are, with no supervision and nothing to do. Even crippled kids; it's all the same.

Most of us were excused from gym because of our disabilities—these kids had all kinds—but when we got in that early, the gym was open, so what we did was invent a game which was known as hockey. It wasn't played with sticks. We had a puck and the idea was you hit the puck toward the goal with whatever you had. Some kids had boots, and some had crutches, and it didn't matter. We had a big thing going pretty soon because there were a lot of kids in that group and we split up into six-man teams. It wasn't long before we had a whole league playing each other every morning. There was one kid on crutches—boy, he was good. I could hop along fast, but he was faster on those crutches than I ever was or would be. I tried to beat him every way I knew and this fellow would just get up on his crutches and—voom! He used the crutch to hit the puck—and sometimes he missed. Once he hit me right on the chin and knocked me out. Boy! That was some guy.

The school people didn't know about any of this, of course, because we played before any of the other students or the teachers got there, but one day one of the boys had a heart attack—he had a bad heart and shouldn't have been playing—and after that we got word to cut out all the hockey. The teachers were afraid we'd break our necks or worse.

After first term high I started selling newspapers on the side and I got a few paper cuts. With stumps like mine that was bad. Blood poisoning set in and I had to go to the hospital for a couple of months. But I did all right in high school in my studies and I had a good time, too. I remember once another student and I, a girl, wanted to see if rabbits multiplied fast as we'd heard they did, so we got two rabbits, and put them together. It was a scientific experiment as far as we were concerned but holy mackerel, you should have heard the teacher of that science course the next morning! You would have thought we were enemy agents. She was ready to send us both to jail or throw us out of school or exile us to the darkest corner of Africa. We were given a severe reprimand and told we couldn't use the laboratory except under supervision after that. They didn't think we were very funny. And we didn't get any extra rabbits out of the deal, either. The two we picked must have been boys.

It was a rough life but there was plenty of fun in it. Just because a guy is handicapped, even as much as I was, doesn't mean you can't do things and you can't laugh and you can't have fun. I had plenty of girls, too; any time I wanted a date, I could get one. Sometimes we'd go back to Coney and take the girls spooning under the boardwalk—after shooting out a few of the lights with a bean shooter. Lights, we figured, were death on romance.

I had some fights. When I was a junior in high school I was helping a guy who had a spot selling papers. A new gang had come in, a gang from Brownsville, and some kid comes up to me—I was about sixteen—and says, "Hey, you, what are you doing here?"

He gave me a shove. I said, "Get lost. I ain't bothering you—don't you try bothering me, and we'll get along good."

He said, "Get lost yourself," and tried to give me a shove. I grabbed him with my arms—they may be eight-inch stumps but they have muscle back of them—and held him in a vise. He was yelling and trying to pull away and a crowd was starting to collect and he grabbed my head and began to bang it against the fender of a car.

What I didn't know was that this guy was part of a gang of young hoods that was muscling in on another gang that worked with the people delivering the newspapers. But as he was banging my head on the car, another car pulled up and grabbed him and whisked off.

Then another fellow came up and told me not to worry any more. "Kid, you're protected," he said to me. "You sell your papers. Get it?"

So I went on selling papers. We had to give a little rebate to some of the boys on the delivery route, but the guy I worked for, who ran that stand, took care of that.

I was delayed in graduating because of the blood-poisoning, so my brother and I graduated in the same term. It was a big deal, all right; my family were there and lots of friends. I had a lot of friends among the teachers; I was secretary of the athletic association and kept the track records and the medical records. I got a great kick out of that. So all the teachers knew me and they were all there. When I got my diploma everyone stood up and whooped and yelled. It was a great kick for me.

After I graduated I began selling the *News* and the *Mirror* at a stand in Brooklyn, between 15th and 16th Street on King's Highway. It was still tough but they didn't bother me, nobody. I did all right. I was making $35 a week, and in those days that was good money. And that was my take-home, after expenses.

Then my folks moved to the Bronx and I was commuting back and forth on the subway. I got pretty disgusted with the commuting and all my social life and everything was in Brooklyn so I took a room alone for the summer. I knew Mom didn't want me to because the draft was getting close to my brother and she didn't want to be alone. But I did it and—well, I just stayed on. But I made a point of seeing her and Dad once a week anyway. Or more.

I had a girl then. She was a nice girl and we went together about five years. I never had any sense of rejection or even special problems socially at that time. I was different physically, but it didn't count. The problem that bothered me was—I had a newsstand but I knew I could do better and I wanted to do better, working somewhere else. Where you work, what you do with yourself in work, that's important, just as important as your social life, or drinking beer. I didn't like the idea of working nights all the time, and the lack of a future. I could sell just so many papers and then I had saturated the area. This to me was not an accomplishment.

So all the time I was selling papers and living by myself I was trying to get a job. A real job somewhere else in some other line. Normal, huh? But when somebody like me walks in, it's different. I would say I could do this job or I could do that job, and the answer would be, "Well, we'll see. You'll hear from us."

But I never heard.

I took some aptitude tests. One of them was to take a lock apart and put it together. I did it just the way we were told but the fellow who was running this test came up and said I was disqualified because I didn't do it. I wanted to show him how I bring the ends of these stumps together and use them just like hands; for something that requires more minute work I always use my teeth. But he wouldn't believe me and he said he didn't have time to watch me do it again. He just said I was a liar.

But I knew the truth. The truth was that nobody

was going to hire me. If there was a dollar to be made, I had to find a way of making it all by myself.

Meantime, life or luck, or whatever you call it, took a hand with that newsstand. The city licensing people changed the bus route, shifted around the whole subway station, built new entrances, and I lost all my customers.

In those newspaper-selling days there were guys who were trying to pull me into the rackets. Hoods that used to tell me, "Alex, you can work with us. Big time, kid. Big dough. Sky's the limit."

All I had to do was pick up betting slips while selling papers. In other words, be a bookie for them. But I turned them down. I didn't want to be marked as such a man. I felt if I ever did that, that would be it for me. I wasn't going to have that kind of life, no matter what else.

I stayed with that even later when I was broke, and some of those guys would see me on the street and come up to me and say, "You're a boob, Alex. You could be making dough."

And I just said, "Sure. Thanks. Never mind."

I'd saved some money, living alone there, almost a thousand bucks, and another fellow and I decided to go into the fluorescent-lighting business. We'd need a car and my dad said he would help us get one. "But it'll have to be fixed up with controls so you can drive it and you have to learn how to drive, Alex," he reminded me.

My buddy and I went down to the Veterans' Administration and saw how they put on all those special devices for disabled veterans but I knew none of them would do for me; we needed a whole new setup. I asked the state people if they would accept a car not just like those used by the Veterans' Administration and some said yes, and some no, and most of them told me, "We'll have to see it first."

Of course, when they saw me, none of them thought I could ever drive anything.

The trouble was, I couldn't see driving in any way with pedals that I had to press down with my stumps. I just didn't figure that would work. I went to several people, including one who was supposed to be tops for making special controls on cars. He couldn't help but as I was going out, a little mechanic came up to me and whispered, "There's a fellow over across town I know. He can fix a car you can drive."

So he gave me this name and when I got there this man knew just what I needed—aluminum things I could rest my stumps on while I drove, and controls on the wheel—a real complicated thing for a guy with no legs and only little pointed stumps for arms to get a setup so he could drive. But he made it so I could get behind that wheel, shift, accelerate, and brake, all with the levers. I found out later he had made a special setup for a man with no legs and trouble with his arms, too. That's why he knew what to do for me.

Before I could learn to drive, I had to get a permit to learn, and I had to take a test to get a permit—and what a test they gave me! I had to drive the car in and out between poles—a regular obstacle course. I did everything perfectly, but when I went to get my permit, the man took my money, filled out the permit, and then stamped it "void."

When I saw this, I blew up. I grabbed the permit right off his desk. "Hey, you, give me that," the fellow behind the desk yelled.

"I bought it; it's mine," I told him, and I ran out of there with my "void" permit and straight to the motor-vehicle commissioner's office.

The commissioner was furious. "If they took your money, they have to give you the test," he said. "You go back and get a permit—and tell them this is an order from me."

Boy, he must have chewed them out on the phone! They were all cursing mad at me for going over their heads. But I got the permit.

With practice, I got so I could handle my car perfectly, but when I took my test the fellow failed me. Not for any good reason. "You parked too far from the curb," he told me, or something like that.

When I went back the second time, the man who was giving the tests took one look at me and the special contraptions in the car and said, "I'm not riding alone with you," and dragged another inspector into the car and off we went. But by then I was all riled up and flunked again, all because I was boiling-over mad.

Those first two tests were up in special areas in the Bronx, difficult places where it was easy to flunk, but the third was in the regular test area and I drove the inspector around quite a bit. I figured if they flunked me again, I was going to appeal straight to the capital in Albany. So I let him know I didn't care what he did. If he wanted to flunk me, all right, but we were going through the test anyway.

So I just went ahead and drove some more, and was

making the U-turn when some stupid guy almost cut us off. I got out of this all right and the inspector didn't say anything. I dropped him off at the motor-vehicle office and waved good-bye to him and drove off. He could have gotten me there and then, because he knew better than anybody I didn't have a license and shouldn't be driving alone.

But two days later there was a thing in the mail. I tore the envelope open and there it was—my license to drive. Boy, oh boy, oh boy! I was a citizen, you know what I mean?

Then, finally, we got down to business—the fluorescent-lighting business, I mean.

Some people just wanted to get rid of me. I got some orders but nothing like enough to be profitable. In fact, the business went down the drain. What with the Korean War we'd figured to have some kind of break because supplies were limited, but it didn't work out that way. We wound up with a bunch of junk that we sold for practically nothing.

This was a dismal period for me. It was like a soap opera. I'd broken up with the girl I'd gone with and thought I loved. I had no money, no business, and Pop and Mom were saying for me to give up living alone and come on home. I had a buddy who was loaning me money and that debt was piling up. I don't think he ever expected it back—but he got it one day.

I had some pretty bad thoughts in those days. I'd tried to get a job every place I could think of and nothing worked out. So I'd think, "Well, I'll give it two more weeks. I'll give it two more weeks and if by Saturday two weeks away I've got nothing—I'll turn on the stove or jump out the window."

I wasn't really kidding but the deadline would come and I'd hang on, still hoping that Monday it would change, something would open up, somebody in business somewhere would understand that I could be useful to him, to his business, that I could do something, maybe a lot more than a lot of bums sitting around and not even trying to do a damn thing.

I really don't think taking your own life is a matter of thinking things out, but I may be wrong. I think it's something that snaps inside you, just like all of a sudden it's too much, everything is too much. You try to get a job and you get turned down, wherever you go you get turned down because you've got no legs or arms. You go into churches and people shake their heads; they're full of sadness for you. You stand on a street corner and somebody tries to give you a handout, a dime or a nickel or a quarter. You have no legs so you're finished; no arms, so you're dead.

What was wrong, what was killing me, was finding out this one thing—that it isn't what has happened to you so much as what other people do to you because you are the way you are. You think these are modern times . . . really you are living in a dead age, ten thousand years ago, when a cross-eyed kid would be thrown off the mountainside because some joker in a mask said the devil put a stamp on him. That, I had learned, was the way we live today, and that was what was tearing me down.

Then one day something happened. A cousin who'd read about it in the papers, wrote a letter to J.O.B.—Just One Break—and asked what they could do for a guy like me, with no legs and no arms? And, sure enough, I got a letter from J.O.B. telling me to drop in and see them. "Alex, you go down there and see them," my cousin said. "Maybe they'll do something, you can't tell."

She knew how low I'd been for weeks and how many places had turned me down and how I felt that no one was going to say yes to me. Maybe she was frightened, too—she may have known how close I was to tossing in the towel. I don't know. But I said all right, I would go—for her. Believe me, I thought so little of it, I was so sure it would be the same old story and the same old turndown, that I went down there in my dirty jacket and I don't even think I shaved. I was that disgusted, that sure nobody on earth wanted me. Not to work.

I got to Bellevue and walked through it trying to find the little office where J.O.B. was located. Finally I got there and saw an interviewer. She was really nice. "There's a place out on Long Island," she told me. "It's just started—it's got just a few people so far, maybe ten or fifteen—they hire only disabled. It's called Abilities, Inc. If you could do anything for them . . ."

What could I do for them? I could work a drill press, for one thing. In spite of myself I was hoping . . . hoping. . . .

"Well, that's the kind of job they've got," she said. "Assembling and packaging and laying in wires and drill presses—all that sort of thing."

Then I got really excited. "Look, I can do it," I told her. "And if I can't now, I can find out how. Whatever they've got, I can do it."

She smiled. "I'll set up the appointment," she said.

I didn't know she'd already called and talked to you,

Hank, and sent along the letter my cousin had written telling how I swam and played handball and even typed despite having no arms. I didn't know you were impressed enough so that you wanted to see me. I didn't know any of that. When I got out there and looked around, the first thing I thought was—I'd like to work in this place. I liked music and there was music playing on the intercom—music piped in—and I liked that. And then I met you—the boss.

If you're like me when you meet people for a job, they're looking up here and down there and everywhere but at you, as though they're ashamed or afraid to look right at you. But there you looked right at me. And I said to myself, "Gee, if this guy is kidding me, he's good." I'd heard about people hiring someone like me and putting them off in a corner somewhere in the factory to work for nothing or practically nothing. And I wondered, "Is he honest about this?"

Here is this fellow looking at me straight and telling me to go out and try this and try that. Could I run a drill press? So I ran a drill press for him. And we went up and down the factory, with him asking me this and asking that, and I picked out jobs I could do and jobs I couldn't. He asked me about laying in wires and lacing and I said, "I don't know but let me take some of those wires and blueprints and things home and I'll come back tomorrow, maybe I can do it. I think I can." I didn't know you didn't have any legs yourself, Hank; I knew you were handicapped but I didn't know just how and I didn't ask. You said, "Well, report back in two weeks and we'll see what we can do." So I started home.

All the way home I'm thinking about this and hoping and not daring to hope either. I knew how some companies used disabled people for door-to-door selling. Like there is some lotion made by the blind and you have to be disabled to sell it. And there are some that sell subscriptions. It's all playing on pity and who wants pity? I wanted a job. And this—this was a job.

How I hoped it was true, what this man promised. I knew I could work the drill press. I looked at the lacing—the wires. I knew that was hard, but I figured with a prong and a hook or something, I could get that all right. And then the packaging. It would have been simple for a guy with hands, but how was I going to do it to meet the standards, to keep up with the others? I had to figure it out. My mind began working on gimmicks and gadgets that might do it. Because you see, as soon as we'd gone into the plant to test out these jobs, I'd begun to think that there might be an opportunity, a real chance, here. But I was afraid to think, too. It was the same thing as with the car and the license. Even when the inspector didn't turn me down, even when I began to think, maybe it might be coming, I wanted it so badly that I didn't dare believe I had it made.

So I go on home and all of this is building up a storm in me like I was going to explore outer space—and when I get to the front door there's a telegram. I pick it up and I hold it for a minute. Then I tear it open—but careful—with my teeth. REPORT TOMORROW TO START WORK IMMEDIATELY. HANK VISCARDI.

Tomorrow! It was almost Christmastime, with the decorations and the stores and the excitement and all that, and the singing. I'm Jewish—my family was

Sephardic—but Christmas is something, you know, warm and meaning something, and now for me it meant a whole new life.

The next day when I went in, I not only had a job, I also had a turkey. Everybody in the shop got a turkey for Christmas and I got mine, too. I went to work on that drill press. I was pretty tense and nervous but I gave it all I had; I wanted to make good in every way I could. And the day I got my first paycheck, you handed it to me, Hank, and you said, "As long as you want to work, Alex, there'll be a place for you here."

That changed everything. As long as I wanted to work! Boy, that would be forever. I was so happy I cried all the way home. I could have got myself killed!

That's how my new life began. But nothing stands still; there's always the dream—you want to be as tall as the next guy.

Right after I got my job I met a wonderful girl. I was very much in love, and now that I had a job, now that my life had begun to take real direction, I was thinking of marriage. And about artificial limbs. I remember, Hank, you said you'd back me in whatever I wanted that way, as a part of Abilities' rehabilitation program —and that's a big part of all this—and so finally I was in the hospital getting operated on so that I could wear artificial limbs.

It was very painful, that operation. I was in a hospital in the country and I lay there in that bed with that pain all the time. And one day you come in. And what do you do? You lean over and kiss me. Me, that tough kid from Coney who'd have clobbered anyone who mentioned the word "sissy," and you said, "Is there anything really troubling you, Alex?"

I said, "Yes."

You said, "Well, what is it? Whatever it is, if I can change it, I will."

I said, "Those damn yapping birds outside the window. Morning, noon, and night they're chirping, chirping, chirping. And I'm lying here and all I can do is listen to them chirp from sunup to sunset. I want to go back to Brooklyn."

You laughed then. "Here we get you a wonderful place in the country, with fresh air and birds chirping and crickets in the night——"

"Those crickets!" I moaned. "All night long trying to get over the birds, I gotta listen to those damn crickets."

Nobody could understand how I could miss Brooklyn when I had all that wonderful disturbance morning, noon, and night. But the truth was, I guess I just felt like complaining about something because of that terrible pain. I was scared, let's face it. Scared of being up that high, all of a sudden . . . scared of getting blood poisoning again if I fell . . . scared of just smashing down somewhere. Because since I had no hands I couldn't walk with a cane. I got nothing going for me. It's like I'm on stilts with nothing to hang onto. When I tried wearing my new legs at the hospital after going through all that, I kept falling.

My girl didn't want me going through all this. She'd come up to see me in the hospital and sit by the bed and tell me, "What does it matter? Why do you want to go through with it? It doesn't make any difference, not to me. I love you the way you are. I don't want you going through all this pain."

You might have thought her family would have been against our marriage, but they weren't. My mother liked her right off—Mom always liked somebody with blue eyes and blond hair. And I got to know her father and mother and we were good friends. When Sue was setting her hair or something and didn't want to go out, her father and I would go and see a movie or have a few belts. He's a wonderful guy, her father is.

In the spring of 1955 we were married, in the rectory of a church in Brooklyn. That was one time I wore the limbs. It was quite a thrill standing up there before the priest—I'm Jewish but my wife is Catholic—with my bride at my side, and you, Hank, behind me, and hearing those words and feeling as tall as the whole world and sure it's all right, the whole thing is going to be all right.

9. Trumpets

"It will be all right," my friend Alex declares, and when Alex says so, that's it.

Alex has come a long way since those early days. He is a supervisor in the packaging department. A miracle man who helps to make the place go. Alex leans on one of those stubby arms and thinks out things—ways of getting the work done better, surer, faster, ways of saving this man or that one from himself, from his own fear, from his own disability.

Alex is a symbol of a place where we know no barrier, where men and women are equal in the opportunity to work as they can, to accomplish as their abilities allow, to live, to play—to pray, to dream, to grow, to achieve, to fulfill.

It will be all right. . . .

And Alex laughs. He laughs and holds one of his two children close to him and he says, "The older one thinks that one day my arms and legs will grow out like everybody else's. But I know she doesn't really think so; she just says it. It is a game with us."

And they laugh.

It is so hard for people to remember that we laugh, we, the disabled. That we are full of the music of laughter that comes with accepting ourselves—and being accepted—on our own terms, for what we are, for what we do.

Arms or legs—or no arms or legs. Or one.

Like Tubby the Incredible. Tubby, who, as a boy in England, lost an arm in an accident; who grew up in Scotland; who lived through the war and the bombings and came to America and tried to get a job.

One-armed people have a difficult time getting jobs! You don't have to be as disabled as Alex to run into trouble. You only have to have just one arm instead of two and the whole deal begins to disappear in glimmering phrases of nothingness: Don't worry. We'll let you know. We'll be in touch with you. There'll be something turning up one of these days. . . .

This is what happened to one-armed Tubby when he tried to get a job in America.

But Tubby, who was married, well-adjusted, and was getting the brushoff from everybody without striking back, had an answer. Tubby had a side line. He loved music. He could sing. He could tell a joke.

When Tubby was a lad, his mother bought a piano so that his sister could learn to play. Tubby sneaked in when no one was around and pretty soon people were saying to Tubby's mother, "I heard your daughter playing today—she does so well."

"But my daughter wasn't home today, only my boy."

"But your boy couldn't have been the one because he only has one arm and——"

"But he was the only one home."

His mother called him in and Tubby sat down with his one hand and played. And from that day on he began to study music seriously. He learned to play the trumpet, and when he was a little older he began giving public performances. During World War II he went on tours, playing for American and British troops, and for them he worked out a routine of playing the piano and the trumpet simultaneously. He mixed in some singing, too, and became, I imagine, the only one-armed trio in all history.

After the war he came to America. He wasn't thinking of a job as a musician, but when he found every other door closed to him he went to the Musicians Union to see about getting a card. At first glance, a pianist with only one arm didn't look promising, but when Tubby was tried out on all the tricky things the examiner could dream up, and did them all, he was made a union member in five minutes flat.

But his union card didn't get him a job, and neither did all the agencies to which he applied. Nobody wanted a one-armed pianist; he was a freak, they said, and who wants a freak at a dance or a concert?

But he registered with all the agencies and kept making the rounds, and one day he got a call. A man who ran a night club in New Jersey was in a terrible spot; he had to have a pianist fast and Tubby's name had come up on the list. "I'll be there," said Tubby.

It was his first real job in America. "All the way out to Jersey on the bus," he told me, "I kept saying to myself. 'What will I do? Will they take to me?' I knew American songs from listening to records and I'd worked with GIs and been at their jam sessions, so I wasn't worried about that. But this was the first time, over here. And maybe when the guy saw me he'd throw me out, anyway.

"So I went to this place, and the boss saw me come in but he didn't notice my arm. So I figure why take a chance by going over there to the boss and saying, 'I'm one-armed.' Or anything else. I just said, 'Hi, I'm the piano player.' And I walk around to the bandstand with my music and throw it there, hoping nobody would look at me. Of course, he might say, the moment he noticed, 'Why did that damn fool agent send you here? How can I use you?' He might say anything.

"But there's a crowd of people out there and I don't say anything except to signal for a spot. And I sit down at the piano and start playing and singing some Irish numbers and some Scotch numbers."

Tubby was scared. As he put it, he was nervous, deep nervous. He had a way of playing, with one hand, sustaining the bass with the foot pedal and playing the treble against the bass pedal, so that it sounded like two hands. He was good enough to fool musicians. A blind one, he told me, asked him about it one day. He wouldn't believe Tubby was playing with one hand until he heard it from Tubby himself.

But to get back to that first night. . . . "They liked me—they liked me a lot. When I finished they clapped and clapped for more and I stayed on longer than I was supposed to, that first night. When I came off for the break, the boss was standing there staring at me.

" 'You're great,' he said. 'You're wonderful. They love you.'

" 'Gee, I'm glad you liked it,' I said. 'I was afraid ——'

" 'Like it? You're a smash. Let me buy you a beer.'

"We were standing at the bar when all of a sudden he looked as if he'd seen King Henry's ghost. 'Where the hell is your arm?'

"Then he realized and he flipped. 'I never would have believed it,' he said. 'Just wouldn't have believed it. I admire you. You're terrific; you're a terrific entertainer.' "

After all his rebuffs, the words were like champagne

to Tubby. "You don't know what you've done for me, saying those words," he said. "That's the real music."

He stayed at the Jersey spot for two months and the word got around. He was signed on as a member of a trio and toured the country for a year. His wife and their young kids were with him, and together they saw more of their new country than most of us do in a lifetime. Then the children were old enough for school, and the time came to settle down, and it was here, to Abilities, that Tubby came. Now he's boss in shipping and receiving.

One arm—or two—or none. One dream or many.

It is not what you seem but what you are, and what you can do.

It is true of Alex and Tubby.

And Phil.

Phil is a severe spastic, with cerebral palsy. Talking to him, you could think that he was mentally retarded, but this is not so. His gait is stumbling and awkward, his speech difficult, his words uttered with grimacing expressions.

But underneath all this is a man—a man with ambitions and dreams, and the raw courage to make them come true.

When you talk to a man like him, there's a simple test that will tell you whether he'll become stable in an environment that provides a satisfactory challenge. Naturally, he's nervous meeting "the boss." His speech gets more difficult and spasticity more pronounced. I used a simple device—and an old one—with Phil. I asked him casually, "Do you happen to have an identification card with you?"

Taking out a wallet and getting an identification card is a familiar thing, an unconscious series of actions. If he's comfortable carrying out the needed motions, he can be stabilized under normal conditions.

You would have been amazed to see with what calmness Phil reached in and drew out his social security card and handed it to me. He had passed the test without a falter.

It was one of our young women employees who became the means by which Phil—with all his grimaces and difficulties—found his way to the most dramatic adventure of his life.

10. PHIL: *Saga of a Man*

I was born a spastic but I never let it interfere with my education, or work, or really with living a full life. You don't have to. But you do have to have courage. That's a big part of it.

When I was very young I used to go to a hospital regularly—for massages. There was some talk about operating on my back but my parents were against it because there's no guarantee—then or now—that you won't come out worse than ever.

I didn't speak very clearly as a kid. I mean, I'm no Lowell Thomas now but then I was, well I had to learn to speak clearly just by practice. I knew the word—in my mind I knew exactly what I wanted to say. But to say it, to make the word sound the way I heard it in my mind, that took time and self-training. I'd go off by myself and I'd say "Cat. Cat. Cat. . . ." Simple words, complex words.

To enunciate more clearly, I would say, over and over again, sentences like "Around the rugged rock a ragged ruffian ran. . . ."

I had a good education. I went to a fine Catholic high school. My marks were all right—around 80 and 85—but I had to work for them, and I was kept after school plenty. I wasn't babied or pampered.

But after I was graduated I found that nobody wanted to employ me, and that was that. I waited around at home, doing nothing for two or three months. Then I decided I would try on my own.

Spastic or not, I got a job. I worked in a gasoline station—twelve hours a day, eight days a week, fifteen dollars a week salary. Pumping gas and parking cars. I didn't have a license to drive, but luckily nobody caught me. I stayed there nine months. Every eight days I had a day off. People were pretty nice to me around Christmastime, I remember. I got quite a few tips.

But I got awfully weary of this job, at that pay. And one night I had—I don't know what you would call it, but I had a dream. And I dreamed that I ought to go down to the State Employment Agency and see somebody down there. I never had a dream like that before, or an experience like that, but it seemed to me very vivid and very real and urgent that I should do this. Not tomorrow or the next day but that very hour. It was still dark outside, in the suburb where we lived. It was around four o'clock in the morning. But I said to myself, all right, if this dream is a way of guiding me, I'll accept that guidance.

I got up in the dark. I dressed myself. I went down

to that office in town. Of course, I was the first when the place opened. The woman who interviewed me said she had a job in a newspaper engraving department, as a messenger. But it was night work—from midnight until eight in the morning. Five nights a week, forty hours a week, forty dollars a week.

It sounded wonderful but I had had too many turndowns before, when I was sent some place and one look at me was the end. I didn't want it this time. So I asked her, "Will you call him, whoever it is who might be going to hire me, and tell him what kind of person I am, before he can take one look at me and say no?"

I listened while she phoned. "I've got a young man who seems bright and willing to work," she said, "but he's a spastic and he asked me to call you and tell you that so that he wouldn't be wasting your time unless you really wanted to talk with him."

"What do I care if he's spastic if he can do the job and wants to do it?" the man said. "You tell him to get up here."

So I had a job.

I stayed on that job for thirteen years and in all that time I missed only one week. I had an attack of appendicitis and an operation. But, surgery and all, I was back at work after only seven days away. I carried cuts and plates and finished engravings, everything like that, but I couldn't see much future, or more money, in it.

Naturally, I wanted to do better for myself if I could and I always was looking around. One day my sister—she's older than I am and married—read about Abilities, and told me about it. I arranged my schedule so I had time to take a trip out there. I talked to Ellen.

She seemed very interested and asked me a lot of questions, and gave me a job application to fill out.

I waited for a month and, when I didn't hear anything, I called her on the phone. "Did you forget about me?" I asked, reminding her of the interview.

I just figured, what did I have to lose? She could only say they didn't want me, and I still had the job at the newspaper, working nights.

But Ellen looked up all the records and said, "Can you come in Thursday for another interview?"

I was there, all right, and this time I got a real job working on cables. With the help of some of the fellows I learned other jobs, and finally wound up with my special section in the wiring department. There I'm doing something creative, something with my hands, and I really like it.

My parents were afraid I was taking a chance. "Why give up a good job you've had all these years for something you don't know about? You don't even know it will work out."

I said to them, "If you want to get ahead, you have to be willing to gamble. And with the help of God, I'm going to try." In the back of my mind, I guess, I had a feeling that this thing was important for me and the Lord would help me do it.

So I started working and getting to know the people around me. Everybody seemed to understand a lot of things that were never put in words and people had fun, no matter who or what they were.

One of them was Naomi. Sometimes I used to have dinner with her. And one evening she said to me, "There's this girl, Diana. I want you to meet her. You might like her. And you might be able to help her."

"How could I help her?"

"She's a polio victim. She got it when she was a little girl and she's lived with it all her life. She was married once, and had two children. Then her husband died. Now she lives all alone, won't go out, and somebody just ought to get her out of herself."

With a chance to help someone else, I agreed. I picked up Diana and we went to Naomi's for dinner and then bowling. I liked Diana but I guess I was bashful. I didn't go back for another date for a long time. Then Naomi invited me to a party. Diana was there and this time we talked more and got to know each other better. After that I called her a couple of times and one time she said, "Phil, why don't you come out for supper?"

After that we dated pretty regularly. We'd go to the movies and out to Naomi's, and we got to know and like each other a lot. She'd been lonely a long time. She'd been a widow for fourteen years and had two grown children—her son was in the Army and her daughter, who lived with her, was nineteen.

Along the line some place I made up my mind that this was the woman for me—the one I wanted to spend the rest of my life with. I hoped she felt the same way about me, and I took a chance. After I'd finished work at the plant one day, I took Diana and her daughter and her niece out shopping. The two girls went into a store and, while Diana and I waited for them outside in the car, I took two rings out of my pocket, held them out, and said, "Which one would you rather have, Diana?"

She looked at the diamonds—and she looked at me. Then she pointed to the one in my right hand. "Phil—I want that one." And she took it, and kissed me.

My parents had known I was seeing Diana, and had met her once, so as soon as I'd slipped the ring on her finger we drove over to my house. Leaving Diana outside in the car—it was hard for her to climb the stairs in her braces—I went in. "Mom . . . Dad . . ." I called out, "I'm engaged."

My dad shook my hand and my mother hugged me, and then we all went downstairs and they made a big fuss over my girl, hugging and kissing her, and wishing her—and both of us—all the happiness in the world.

But it's a funny thing about parents, particularly the parents of the disabled. The strong and the whole leave the nest—or are pushed out of it—and that seems only natural. Mothers have a reputation of crying at their kids' weddings, of course, but that stuff about losing a son, or a daughter, isn't taken very seriously by any of them.

With the disabled, it seems to be different. Though they liked Diana, and had seemed so happy at first about our engagement, within a few days they had cooled off on the whole thing. They had all sorts of reasons, the way parents always do, and—I guess as children always do—I had all sorts of answers, and I couldn't understand why they couldn't understand my point of view, and they were just as sure they were doing and saying the right thing for me.

If I'd been smarter, or more experienced, I'd have known that this was only their way of trying to protect me, as they had all my life. Dimly, I guess, I did know this, but I knew I had to make up my own mind: Was I going to stay in the nest where I'd been cared for all my life, or was I going to make the break? To be a man, standing on his own two feet, setting up his own home, caring for a wife of his own and being loved and cared for in return?

I've learned since that I wasn't the only person at Abilities with the same problem—and I won't be the last. I only knew it was a difficult decision I would have to make. And I made it.

Perhaps to every disabled person, in different ways, there comes the moment of decision. Are you to remain forever the helpless, sheltered individual, relying entirely on others, in the home, the family, the institution, with security guaranteed because you have a disability and society will take care of you therefore, or will you free yourself from any bondage you can, within the scope of the abilities you still have; will you have the courage to stand on your own two feet, real or artificial, to take hold of your cup of life, even with convulsive hands?

All this was in my mind as I weighed the question of which way I had to go. Because we are inward-looking, people sometimes forget that everybody faces similar problems in their lives, in one way or another, all people, able and disabled alike.

I closed the door on the place I'd always called home—and persuaded Diana to schedule our wedding just as soon as we could make the arrangements.

It was a tiny wedding, that Saturday morning in the little church on Long Island. My bride's son and daughter were there, and my brother-in-law and sister-in-law. There was nobody from my family.

But when we got home from the church, the neighbors had arranged a buffet and a party. I said my thanks awkwardly while Diana beamed from her chair and we went off on a twenty-four-hour honeymoon as happy as if we'd been married in St. Patrick's and had a big blowout at the Waldorf.

On Monday morning I was back at Abilities, hard at work. I had a family to support now. I was a man.

There was a time when I wouldn't have believed that all this was possible. I was the crippled child, I was the spastic with the gnarled movements. Who could love someone like me? How could I hope for a good job, for a happy life, for fulfillment?

And all of it now has come true. I used to pray about it. I prayed about it and it came true.

I think I have an angel. . . .

It has been a wonderful marriage, really. I disagree with the old idea that two disabled persons shouldn't marry. I think it's wonderful to know that my wife understands me and my problems as I understand hers. Not only our problems, but inner glintings and yearnings that have special meaning to us.

Last Christmas we decided to do a special thing; we would take a foundling into our home for the Christmas holidays. So we had it all arranged and Diana's niece was to go over and pick up the little girl and bring her here to our home, and we set up a beautiful Christmas tree and decorated it with ornaments, and then we waited for the niece to return with the four-year-old girl named Kathleen.

Well, when the little girl arrived, she just stood there in the doorway and looked in wonderment at that tree, with all the lights and ornaments, and then, to my amazement, she ran to Diana and put her arms around her knees and called her "Mommy."

It was a wonderful weekend. The weather was terrible and we stayed in the house and played and talked and laughed together.

But the highlight was Christmas morning, when we waited for the little one to wake up and then we all went in together and crowded around the tree and there were presents underneath—most of them for Kathleen—and we opened our Christmas presents. And we had Christmas dinner later with turkey.

It was just for the weekend of course and it was over on Tuesday morning and there were tearful partings and promises to be together soon again.

And we will, I promise her that.

11. Visitor

We are not what we seem; we are what we are. But there are differing ways of looking at us, at Gale, Peter, Ellen, Naomi and me. It depends so much on who you are, and what you are, and from what vantage point you look.

They go back to the work bench outside my office. It is not a bench really; it is a vision; it is not one bench, but many; no one job but many: It is four hundred human beings at work helping to build for a nation they live in, for a world they make as much theirs for their contribution as any other workers in the universe.

Naomi goes back and merges into the work of this day. The sunlight filters through the skylights and in the light and shadow her fingers move with speed and dexterity, wires gliding into place, yellow and red and green merging into predesigned position as part of a component of modern electronic calculation.

A visitor stands behind her watching. He is being shown through the plant by one of my assistants—Ray, the pianist. He is a visitor here from Honolulu who heads up a new group for the blind out there. A former newspaper man who lost his eyes as a correspondent in the front lines in Korea, he has come to see what we do and how we do it. Ray tells me later, "You know, he is the only blind man who has learned to fly a plane and has a license. Of course, he has to have a co-pilot. . . ."

There are many visitors to Abilities. Groups from foreign countries—Scandinavia and Southwest Asia, India and Turkey and Yugoslavia, and groups of many kinds from America. People who did not believe that men can work at such jobs as we have, packaging for great companies, building components of aircraft, and electronic devices, machining complicated parts—all of the business that goes into modern electronics.

We even had, on one occasion, a group of some fifty postulant nuns—young women preparing to be nuns. I had been honored by a special invitation from their Mother Superior to lecture to them about our work and to show them colored slides, and they had been so excited by the ideas in Abilities that they came as a group, to see and ask their questions.

Visitors come to observe. They come afraid that they will turn away in revulsion, in pity, in fear, in whatever it is that grips them and say, "Oh, I pity you, my brother, but I do not dare to look upon you."

But when they get here they do not turn away. For what they see are not the cripples they expected, but fellow human beings at work, people who, like they themselves, have disabilities of one sort or another, but who also have abilities and high skills that can meet the competition in the highest-skilled operations of our times.

Suddenly you see in the faces of the visitors a change, a sense of awareness that has not been there before. Why, these are people like me, they seem to be saying. Why did I never stop to realize before that it was not my pity they wanted, but a chance not to be different, not to be eliminated from the human race long before their time was due? Why did I not realize that it was not misery and tears they wanted, but understanding, opportunity—a chance to work and a chance to live?

All of this you see in the wordless wonder of some of the visitors.

Visitor

Standing behind Naomi, watching, looking over the workers along that part of the line in the plant, is a visitor of another kind. He is a man in his mid-forties, married, with a family. In the branch office of Abilities we have established in Florida, George has become one of my star halfbacks on the executive staff, fighting to establish a new direct mail advertising business as part of the Florida operation.

"Hello, Hank," he says, "I just got in. My plane just landed."

George is here for a series of business conferences. We know it will be a tough fight to get the direct mail department moving; the whole Florida operation has been a hard fight against every kind of obstacle. But we are used to battles; we grow strong on problems; we grow in the struggle and we build our triumphs on the steppingstones of our defeats.

He comes to me, on his crutches and heavy braces, and we shake hands.

I remember when we first saw him, and his first job there.

And so this crutch-carrying, brace-wearing man from the sunlight of Florida told me of another tropical world ten thousand miles away and a young seaman on a PT boat in Lingayen Gulf.

12. GEORGE: *The Island*

It was in the Philippines, in World War II. I'd enlisted in the Navy back in Hartford, my home town, and I'd chased my squadron all the way from Hartford to the Admiralty Islands in the South Pacific and finally to the Philippines, in Lingayen Gulf. I was on duty there on a PT boat; patrolling, mostly, taking patrols into enemy-held spots.

None of it was rugged—until the day I felt sick. I didn't know what it was, but I knew I must have fallen asleep on watch and asked the skipper if I could make sick call and he said O.K. When I got to shore on this typical Philippine jungle island, I found the Navy hospital—it was a tent big enough for about eight people. The doctor was a young jg lieutenant. I told him I felt tired and weak. He took my temperature, looked at the thermometer and said, "Well, you're not running a fever, anyway."

Then he started asking me questions. How long I'd been out and like that. "How many patrols have you made?" he asked.

When I said it was about thirty or forty, he said, "I'll bet you'd like to go home."

That was in 1945; I'd been in service eighteen months.

"I don't think there's anything really wrong," he said. "Go back to your boat."

So I did. All that day I felt pretty awful. Then I had liberty and I got six cans of beer and went into a little shack on the dock and began drinking beer. A little later, I went into a place that had been fixed up as a shower.

Of course the water was cold and when I got out, I got the worst chill I ever had in my life. A couple of fellows looked at me and said, "Boy, you look peaked. You'd better get the hell out of here."

I decided I'd better go back to sick bay, to that tent. I didn't know if it was the beer or what. When I walked in, there was the same doctor and when he saw me he asked, "Weren't you here this morning?"

I said, "Yes, sir."

He took my temperature again. He said, "I think you better stay here. We'll take a malaria smear." Just casual-like. I got myself a cot, took off my dungarees and stretched out. I sat up a little later and wrote my mother a letter, because I remembered I hadn't written her in a long time and I thought, suppose something serious happens to you and you can't write, she'd be scared not hearing. So I wrote, but of course I didn't say that anything was the matter with me.

They took the malaria smear the next morning and after a few hours the jg came back and said: "Well, you don't have the malaria bug, anyway. That's something."

He seemed pretty cheerful so I felt there was nothing seriously wrong with me. About half an hour later I had to go to the head—the toilet—which was really nothing but a trench dug out behind the tent. I made it out all right but on the way back my knees gave out, and I fell. There was a corpsman only a few feet away from me and when he saw me start down, he grabbed me under the arms and asked, "What's the matter?"

I said, "I don't know. I must have tripped or something."

I tried to stand but I couldn't. The corpsman and some other fellow got me back to bed. I felt stiff and numb but that was all. No pain, no real pain, no sense of paralysis. Just stiff and numb and my legs wouldn't hold me up. They left me on the cot. About two o'clock that afternoon I had to urinate. And I asked them, the people around me, if I could have a duck or could somebody help me to the latrine?

I tried to throw my legs over the side of the cot and I couldn't. I was afraid even to try to stand. So someone brought me the duck and I tried to use it. I sat up and I lay back and I tried to urinate and I couldn't. I told the corpsman, "I want to and I can't."

"We'll have to catheterize you," he said.

They put a hose up you so you could go. It happened hundreds of times afterward but that was the first time, and it was quite a shock. Then this jg doctor was back, asking me questions. Everything under the sun. You would have thought I had stolen the admiral's private stock. Then he said, "There're a lot of boys coming in here. Tomorrow we'll have to move you."

I said, "What's the matter with me?"

I was just a kid, a seaman second class on that PT. I'd never been sick before and I was scared and this doctor just didn't seem to know what was the matter. I was plain scared, that was all.

The next morning some corpsmen, all with masks on, picked me up, cot and all, and moved me to another tent, the kind you might use on a camping trip, and I was alone. If I wanted anything I had to yell like hell. One corpsman came in that day and I said, "What the hell is the matter with me?"

"Don't tell the doctor I told you," he answered, "but what you've got is spinal meningitis."

I knew something about meningitis, and how it could kill you, or leave you mentally retarded. And as I lay there all alone I had nothing to do except think about it—and about the fact that there I was, right at the edge of the squadron area, just where a sniper might sneak in with a bullet.

At night, it was even worse, with the noises—the locusts and the sort of sizzling sound of the jungle. I was plain scared and I'd yell for somebody to come, but nobody ever did. I was there, I think, four nights, and every night it was pure hell.

The days weren't much better. When I tried to urinate again, I couldn't. "I'll have to have that hose put in me, or something," I told the corpsman. "I can't stand this. I'm bursting inside. Help me, for God's sake! Get something, do something!"

I was in terrible pain, and excited. The corpsman

said, "Well, the doc's not here right now. He's gone to lunch and then he said he was going to play volley ball this afternoon. Unless there's an emergency——"

I said, "Can't you help me?"

"I can't. The doc has to do it."

"Will you get him?"

"Yes," he said, "I'll get him."

Three hours later that doctor showed up to cathetérize me. When he came in I must have used some vulgar language and I must have been crying because he was quite upset. I remember his words as if they were engraved on a plaque of high medical standards. "You won't die. A little pressure on your tummy won't kill you."

A couple of days later he came in with a pin. Just a common pin like you take out of a new shirt. By this time I couldn't move my legs. I couldn't even wiggle my toes. I could feel everything, all the way up from the bottom of my feet. I was ticklish but I couldn't move. He rubbed his fingers on my feet. "Can you feel this?" he asked. "Now, move, move." And he started pricking the bottom of my feet with the pin. "Move," he kept saying.

I said, "Doc, I can't move a thing. Stop it."

I was crying again. I remember crying when he did it.

Then he started asking me more questions. "Did you enlist in the Navy or were you drafted?"

I told him I enlisted.

"Do you like the Navy?"

"Yes."

"Would you like to go home?"

"Yes."

He said, "Aw, you'll be all right. We'll take care of you. Don't worry about it."

Gee, the way he said it, for a moment I felt good. But right after that, as he got up to leave, he took out a package of matches, struck one, swung around quickly and stuck it to the bottom of my foot.

I let out a cry of pain, and really told him off.

He turned around and walked out.

The next day a flight surgeon attached to a squadron of PBY patrol Catalina bombers—the Black Cats, they were called—came in and ran some more tests. Then two other doctors came in, along with that jg doctor and the commander at the base. The commander asked me a lot of questions and did the pin act again—but no more matches. He seemed decent and more humane than the others. Like he figured I was a human being.

I wasn't thinking very clearly that day but I knew they were talking about me and I heard the commander say, "Well, it's possible but it would be hard. You stuck him, you used the pin, you used the match."

The jg said, "Yes, but I still have some doubts."

I spoke up. "Commander, what's wrong with me? Why won't my legs hold me? Why can't I go to the john?"

"Son," he said, "I think you have infantile paralysis." He paused. "You know, like President Roosevelt."

"Is it going to last a long time?" I asked him. "Will it go away?"

He said, "Well, don't worry about that now."

The next day my crew showed up and our skipper. "Hello, George," he said. "It's Bob."

"I guess I'll be here a while," I told him. "No more trips on the PT. Not for a while."

"Don't worry, George," he said. They were all trying to sound cheerful but I knew, inside, they were thinking that I wasn't coming back. Not to the PT anyhow. I knew it no matter what they said.

But the Skipper was wonderful. He and the boys from the PT stood around at the entrance to the tent and talked and kidded and told me the damn fool things that had happened on the last patrol. I started laughing and kidding with them the way we had always done. It was a real wonderful visit.

Although I didn't know it until I got home, the skipper wrote my mother right after that, telling her all about their visit to me, and that I seemed to be getting along great; that I was laughing like my old self again.

Right after that I got moved out in an Army truck. First I was taken to a church that was being used as a hospital. It had been bombed so badly that all that was left was four walls. There was a canvas cover to keep out the rain, and Filipino priests would come in sometimes to say Mass.

After a few days I got moved farther back of the lines to an Army evacuation hospital where there were nurses, not corpsmen. There were more examinations and tests and I kept hearing the word polio.

I had been sick for seventeen days and I had not defecated once in all that time. I had terrible cramps; an enema didn't work; and the pain was so awful I thought I would die. Finally a doctor performed what they called an "extraction." It took more than an hour to clean me out. It was pure hell.

After that they kept me mostly on fluids.

Everybody was good to me in this hospital, doctors

and nurses. They moved me out of isolation after a time and I was with other guys in the ward. Then one day an Army ambulance pulled up and they put me on a stretcher. They had a bottle and one of those tubes for catheterizing me and they told me, "If you want to go, tell the nurse and she'll flush you."

There was already one patient in the ambulance and while they were putting me in, he asked, "What's wrong with him?" When the driver told him it was polio, but noncontagious, the other patient nearly hit the overhead. "What the devil do you mean, putting a polio in my ambulance?" he demanded.

It seems he was a captain and he didn't want me to ride with him even though there was room for four.

But I did.

We went to the airfield and were flown to Leyte, where there was another hospital. I thought I was going back to America but they said, "Oh, no, you've got to go to isolation."

"I've been in isolation for weeks," I said. "How can I still be contagious now? And if I am, how come they're flying me around like this, so I can infect everybody from the plane crew to the guys on the airstrip and all the other patients flying with me?"

Didn't matter. I was in isolation again for fourteen days.

Then, finally I was put on a ship and sent back to America. I came into San Francisco on a carrier and, with all the other guys, was taken up to the flight deck so we could see the Golden Gate and the bridge. There was a band at the pier and a reception committee, and I was lowered in one of those baskets and put into another ambulance. I'll never forget the ride from the ship to the San Francisco Receiving Hospital. The crazy driver drove like it was the last trip to hell. I thought to myself, "It took me all this time to get here and now he's going to kill me between the ship and hospital."

But we made it and the hospital people gave us lunch. By now I could eat some solids. Then we were told, "If anyone wants to make a phone call, we'll bring the phone right to your bed."

I thought, if I call mother, she is going to be terribly upset. And yet I knew I ought to call. And oh, how I wanted to!

I lay in bed thinking I ought to call, but not being able to make up my mind until finally, late in the afternoon, I picked up the phone and gave the operator my family's number in Hartford, Connecticut.

I was still a kid and all of this polio business was a shock. I didn't know where it would lead to or what I'd be like or what I could do. I'd been pretty close to my dad always, but when you're that young—I was just out of my teens, remember—you are sort of closer to your mother. I suppose that was it. Anyway the moment I got through, the moment I heard her say, "Hi!" well, I broke up. I guess a lot of guys did that sort of thing so I wasn't alone. And she said right away, "George, do you want me to come out there?"

And I said, "No, Mom. I'll be coming back East pretty soon. I don't know how soon, Mom, but it won't be long anyway."

I wanted her to come so badly, so badly, but I kept saying, "No. They're going to send me to Boston. They told me they're sending me to Boston."

I talked to them all, to Dad and my brother, and—

you know how we Italians are, Hank—there was a lot of talk and tears over the phone, but it was good and I said I'd be seeing them all before they knew it.

But it was longer than I thought. My next stop was at Oak Knoll, in Oakland, across the bay from San Francisco. There I landed in "The Hill," where people with mental disorders were sent. And I found out this was because that jg doctor out in the Philippines had put a notation on my record that I was a psychopathic faker pretending to have a disease I didn't have at all! I had been diagnosed as having polio by the best experts. I was paralyzed and couldn't walk. I had been given every scientific test in the book, and yet I was forced to go through daily tests because of that one doctor's notation.

I have to give them credit for being thorough. Believe me, if any goofball could pull a fake with that kind of examination, he ought to get the Pulitzer prize and an Oscar besides, because he would have to be a genius at acting.

Everyone was good to me at "The Hill" while I was being tested and having long daily talks with the head psychiatrist. I had a room by myself, got mail, was allowed to have visitors. An Army guy I knew came with his wife to see me and later they called home for me to find out how things were. They came back the next day and told me my dad had a heart attack. It was a terrible shock, even though they said he was pulling out of it. The nurse bawled out my friends for telling me, but I was glad I knew.

I myself was coming along, physically. I could get to the head on my own if someone helped me into a wheelchair. I was taking baths in the Hubbard tank and pulling weights; in fact, my upper torso at that stage was fine.

As I got better I was moved into a ward and was allowed out to the movies—in a wheelchair. A lot of the other fellows were out on liberty twenty hours out of twenty-four, but most of the time I was in the sack. Mom sent me some pajamas and sitting around in them and a robe made me feel good. It was all right. I had the feeling I was getting well. Then I got word I was being sent to another place in California, Corona. I was furious but the doctor explained that the hospital there had good equipment, and chances were if I went there I'd soon be up and around.

In those days I never even thought of braces. I figured I'd walk like anybody else. Nobody ever said I wouldn't. In fact this guy, this psychiatrist, said, "What the hell are you worried about? If you don't make out too well, you'll be well compensated."

That's what he thought was important to me!

So I went to Corona. More doctors. About forty-five other polio guys, all of us patients. One great doctor I had—Commander Chamberlain from Colorado, a wonderful man who gave me back myself, physically and spiritually. "You will walk, in one way or another—but you will walk," he said to me once. "And you will walk, George, just as far as you have the vision and the courage. The polio will leave its scars. But some of them—many of them—you can overcome. Do you understand me?"

After I was there for some months, I got a thirty-day leave. I was able to go home. It would be the first time

I had seen my parents since I was taken ill and I thought I would surprise them so I didn't let them know I was coming East. But a woman I was talking to on the plane said I couldn't just go in like that, with no announcement. "You have to send word ahead," she said, and she got the pilot to send word to Hartford.

When I got to Hartford, there was the family—my mother and Dad and my two brothers—at the station. I guess I didn't really want them there, to see me, a cripple with a brace and two big wooden crutches.

I wanted to act big, grown up, and I took a couple of bottles of whisky out of my suitcase and said, "Here, Dad, a present I brought for you."

I don't know what he must have thought—what kind of creature had come home. Those thirty days weren't so good because I kept trying to prove myself to them and to me. Once I fell down on the pavement and my mother came rushing down the stairs to help me. I guess I was pretty cold to her and I said, "Just leave me alone, Mom. Leave me alone." And I picked myself up and went on down the street.

All the relatives had to come to see me, too. You know how Italian relatives are. I never saw so many in all my life. Neighbors, too. They would come in and weep a little bit and then they'd go out.

Some of the people from school—the coach and some of the boys—came over, and they were different. I didn't mind talking to them; they seemed to understand better. And those who didn't understandstand made me feel as if I were dead or at least that for me life was over.

Everyone meant well, I realize now, and some of

them are still near and dear to me. I know now how they felt. But right then, that first thirty days, it was rugged and I was glad to get back to California where I was learning how to live again.

I was there a year. Many of my friends were being sent home. My best friend, who used to take me out in my wheelchair, was discharged. I began to wonder if I'd have to stay there forever.

I talked to the doctor about Warm Springs. "Sure you can go there," he said, "but right now they're jammed up. The only way to get in is to know somebody who can write a letter—somebody with some influence."

Back home I knew a congressman, and I'd worked for his brother as a newsboy. I called home and had my family get in touch with him, and three days later —just three days—I was on my way to Warm Springs. There I was fitted with braces on both legs. They weighed a ton. But I was all set.

Then I went home. I was out of the Navy. I was out of hospitals. I was out of Warm Springs. Physically— and mentally—I had adjusted. I wasn't mad at the world, I wasn't angry about what had happened to me. I wasn't even sore at that lieutenant jg doctor who had tried to get a mental disturbance note on my record— there wasn't any on it when I walked out.

The rest is not so different from what happens to the average person, and that's perhaps the most exciting thing about it. That fall I went to Bryant College, in Rhode Island. There I met Brev and right away—after our first date—I knew I was in love with her. Luckily, she felt the same about me. After we were married, we went to California and I took some courses in business administration and radio—I thought for a while I'd like to be an announcer. But we were both homesick, so we headed East, stopping off in Mississippi to visit her folks, and winding up in Hartford. I worked there for two years in a city job, doing general clerical work and operating a PBX machine. Then, in the fall of 1952, I resigned and Brev and I and our eighteen-months-old baby, Steven, took off for Florida.

Getting a job is never easy for a guy in my shape, but I had some training and some experience, and I landed one as a bookkeeper with a fuel company. I was glad to get it at the time—but like everyone else, I had a dream. And when I got a chance to work with Abilities I grabbed it.

None of this sounds extraordinary, I know—it's the kind of thing that happens to most guys starting out on their own. By me, that's what makes it so great. Braces or no braces, I'm living like people.

I have three children and like most men who go away on business, I bought a surprise present the other day for my little daughter—a dress. I rode up on the department-store escalator to the little-girl's dress department and I got a lot of funny looks. But I like riding on escalators. And I wanted to buy Karen a dress.

The good happens, and the tragic, too. In 1952, about eight or nine months after we moved there, my mother and dad and brother drove down to visit us. Dad liked Florida; he thought it was great. And I never saw him looking so good. For one week he looked like a king.

Then he had a stroke—just like that, and passed away, there in Florida, while he was visiting us.

You might expect Mother would have said, "Well, if he just hadn't come all this distance to Florida, the first time since World War I he'd been out of Connecticut, maybe it wouldn't have happened." But she didn't. Instead, she said she had never seen Dad so happy in his life as that last week, with all of us together, and that we could all be glad we shared that time and that happiness with him.

So some of it is good, and some bad, and the battle in Florida to put over Abilities, Inc., down there, and to get this new direct mail department going at high speed—is rough. But as far as I'm concerned it's living and trying and doing and sometimes winning, for your wife, your family, your boss, the people around you.

It's a whale of a lot to have going for you, for a guy like me.

13. Reasons

Whether it's a boy stricken on a far-off island or in the heart of his family, surrounded by those who love him most, the dream is always there, and at Abilities the goal is to make the dream come true.

A young man came to us not long ago with a serious heart condition. He was just twenty-two years old, but our physicians, after examining him, said they had never seen a heart condition so serious as this. The youth might collapse at any moment, they told me—on thc job, on his way to work. "He cannot live more than a few weeks at the outside. How can he go to work for you? Let him go home to bed and let him die."

I thought about this a long time, in the silence of my office. I prayed about it, too. And I decided finally—or was led to decide, I believe—to let this youth come to work. Let him have this chance to use what abilities he had, for as long as he could. I talked with his mother about it and she agreed that he had a right to this much happiness, this much meaning to his life.

So he came to work for us. He worked on the bench, in a wiring job. Several times he collapsed; once, after he'd come to work in the bitter wintry cold, the nurses and staff in the plant infirmary had to work over him.

But they revived him and he kept on working. He remained a member of our staff and one of the best workers in our wiring department. Then one morning we had a phone call: He had died in his sleep.

But his mother had a special message for Abilities. "I want you to know, Mr. Viscardi," she told me, "that the last weeks of his life were the happiest he had ever known. You let him be a part of the world, you let him contribute—through Abilities—in the way any young man likes to contribute, with the work of his hands and mind.

"I want to thank you for the opportunity you gave my son in these last six weeks and for the happiness he found."

It is most certainly true that the hiring and employing policies of Abilities, Inc., are unique. The standards are not far different from those at other plants. The aged who are still able and eager to work, the sick, the weak, the diabetic, the heart-ridden—if they can work, there is a chance for them here. When all the world says no, they may get a productive chance—here.

One day I received a phone call from a high executive in another company. "Hank," he said, "I have a man here I'd like you to talk to. He's a fine worker, expert with figures, a certified public accountant, and has a first-rate business mind."

"What's wrong with him?"

"Well, Fred's over age, for one thing, and you know how a big firm like ours has to run right by the book. And he is, in addition, blind in one eye. But that goes back a long time—like half a century."

"And he doesn't want to quit now?"

The executive laughed. "Hell, he says he'll outlive and outwork all of us."

He sounded like a perfect candidate for Abilities, Inc.—overage, blind in one eye, and eager at his age and with his disability not to rest, but to work.

Fred had himself a ball telling his story. He'd been a

big-league pitcher for a little while, back at the turn of the century. He'd pitched on his college baseball team in California, and a scout for the New York Giants, at that time in spring training in Los Angeles, heard that the kid had pitched a couple of no-hitters. So Fred became a Giant, and the day he arrived at the field where the club was working out, a big man came over. "I'm going to break you in, son. I'll help you any way I can and we'll see if we can get you ready. My name is Christy Mathewson."

So Fred went to work for the "Big Six" as they called him, and Mathewson—perhaps the greatest pitcher in the history of baseball—told him, "You've got as much speed as anybody in the business. All you need is control."

They worked on control for weeks. Fred met John McGraw, the famed manager of the Giants, and Honus Wagner, and many others of the great in baseball. His first season he had one win and one loss to his credit. The next year—in 1907—he was ready to take a regular place on the Giant pitching squad. The team had played only four games, when, in St. Louis, he tossed up a few in batting practice.

"Christy had just given me word that I was ready to start games and I was throwing up a few before this game and the batter—funny, he happened to be a man who was deaf and dumb, they called him Dummy Taylor—he hit a grounder back to me. It hit a rock and bounced right into my eye. I saw more stars than you've ever seen in your life!

"I got on my feet O.K. but they sent me to the hospital for a few days' observation. I knew I wasn't in any shape to play ball for a while, but it wasn't until two months later I knew I was blind. I went to Johns Hopkins, where my brother was an assistant to the famous Sir William Osler and knew all the famous men on the staff. They examined me and said, 'Leave it alone. If you try an operation you might affect the other eye. You've still got one good one.' "

For fifty years, Fred used that good one and became one of the top accountants in his firm. When I learned of the high caliber of his performance from the industry which was ready to retire him, I told him, "You've got a job here. We need additional accounting facilities and an expanding accounting program to meet our growing operations."

Result: Fred, half-blind, overaged, ready for the industrial pasture, not only came into Abilities but has risen to become controller of the firm and one of our key executives.

Len is a younger man, with a heart condition. He has what they call mitral stenosis. He also has a wife and three children, the oldest about ten. When the first attack came, five years ago, he was hospitalized for months and a fellow patient told him about Abilities. After he was well enough to work, he came out to the plant. There were some who said that work at the plant would kill him, even specially set up jobs that he could do without great strain, but he wanted to work—he wanted to pay the bills for himself and his family, and he wanted to live. The amazing thing was that the more he worked, the stronger he got.

One night, after four years, he developed a serious

nose hemorrhage. The whole staff, from my secretaries and I on down, pitched in, phoning special doctors and St. Francis Hospital, and moving into high gear. Speedy action, we knew, was the only chance of saving his life.

When we got the hospital on the phone, we didn't ask if they would take Len; we told them the ambulance was on its way. Everyone on the staff was galvanized into action. There was no hysteria, no duplication; wheelchairs and canes and crutches rolled in this emergency teamwork as we got Len into the ambulance. He was there—at an eighty-mile-an-hour clip—in a matter of minutes.

Len sent me a note from the hospital. Speaking of the "disabled" crew of Abilities, he wrote:

"Their quick action and teamwork and stay-with-it spirit, the nasal packs, the ice, the running around to help, the ambulance, the quick trip to the hospital, and especially the reassuring hands and the comforting words of faith the gang offered, all these combined are perhaps the reason for my being able to write you this note.

"Hank, you can lecture about it, you can write about it, as you have, you can show it on film, but unless you really live in this quiet jungle of determination and unless you feel the results of its drive and the motivation, it still appears impossible and unbelievable the way people at Abilities take things like this in stride.

"The nosebleed was caused by high blood pressure. It's encouraging to note that a study of the heart and lungs shows absolutely no worsening of the condition which originally brought me to Abilities. The condition is unchanged even after four years of active work, when they said I would never be able to work. The doctors here tell me never to give up my determination because that is the one factor that fools the predictions.

"But there's another factor without which it wouldn't have happened either. You, Hank. . . . And that unbelievable gang to whom I owe my life. . . ."

Hands and hearts and legs and eyes. And the strength and courage of men to meet adversity. Each is its separate story, its private moment of drama. Even in defeat, even in loss, as with the youth who was with me so briefly—but I think so importantly—it was a kind of special triumph.

There are other kinds of victories, garish and harsh in their drama. Stories that the world does not hear. And yet, should they be forgotten, should they be untold, if they show what human beings can and will go through for a chance at life, for a chance to hold on, for the opportunity to help someone they love?

Should we forget about Irene because some people may turn from her story? Blindness bothers them, perhaps. Let her son save her sight if he can. Let him speed through the night on that wild trip. Let that crazy gang at Abilities worry about it.

Dare anyone say, "Don't bother me with anything so harsh, so melodramatic, so tear-ridden as this"?

Or should we listen to the story of Irene as she told it to me?

14. EYES FOR IRENE

I was born in Athens, Greece, in 1901. Born blind. My mother died at my birth, and my father came to America a few years later. I lived with my grandmother and my uncle until I was eight and my father sent for me. He had remarried, so I had a stepmother and a half-sister.

My father took me to many doctors for treatment and I gained some of my sight. My father didn't know about schools for the blind, so I went to public school for a year or two, until I nearly lost all my sight again.

You see, my father didn't think of me as blind; he didn't want to face that. The school authorities told him I should go to a school just for the blind. The one I attended was a boarding school and taught many things I wouldn't have learned in regular schools . . . like playing the piano. After I finished high school I studied physical education and then got a position in the Maryland School for the Blind in a little town just outside of Baltimore.

I spent two years there. When I came back to New York, I worked for a time taking care of a child—I still had some vision. Then I met a young man and we fell in love and were married and moved out to Sheepshead Bay where our two children were born. My husband was blind. He ran a vending stand, a newsstand, and later had a concession in a building on Whitehall Street in New York.

We did all right, I guess. We had two normal, wonderful kids, whom neither of us could see. My vision was—well, it was there but it was almost nonexistent. My son and daughter grew up, and then my husband died and I was alone. We didn't have much money; the children were grown, with children of their own, and I didn't want to be a burden on them. I worked for a branch of the Lighthouse in Long Island City. Then a neighbor told me about Abilities. She said it was run by a Mr. Viscardi. A man from the Industrial Home for the Blind brought me out to the plant. It was just getting started at that time, in 1952.

I remember Artie, who's now the executive vice-president, met me at the door and said, "Go to work." It was all sort of spontaneous at that time. They needed people on those newfangled wiring setups they were just starting and there I was. I could always do a lot with my hands and I used bobby pins on the boards to show me where this or that wire was. There were eleven men working in the whole place then—and I was the first woman.

Then I went into packaging. That was when I met the doctor—Dr. Hughes, the ophthalmologist. He said to me, "You know, you might see, Irene, one day."

I said, "I know. I might."

"Really, I mean it," he said. "Did you ever hear of a corneal transplant?"

I had heard something about it, but not in any detail. Dr. Hughes explained that in my case what he wanted to do would be a very delicate operation, because it would involve transplanting to my eye a cornea from someone who had just died. He planned to try it in one only, but he said that would give me greatly improved vision.

The timing, he said, made the process very difficult. "You have to have someone who leaves his eyes for this purpose and the moment he dies the cornea has to be removed and the operation done almost immediately thereafter so that the tender tissues will live and survive when transplanted to the living person."

Everybody at Abilities was as excited as I was at the thought of this operation because Dr. Hughes had said, "Yes, I can transplant a cornea to your eye and I think it will work."

He also said, "I want to know where you are all the time—because you can never tell when this moment will come and you have to be prepared to move very fast."

I gave him the phone number of Abilities, and my own home number, and my daughter's. She was married then and had a little girl of her own. But my son was still single and living with me.

Everybody always knew where I was, most of the

time anyway, but one Saturday I went out shopping and that was just when the doctor called. "We have a cornea, we think," he told my son, "and may have to do this operation on your mother quickly. Where is she?"

All my son knew was that I was out shopping. It had just never occurred to me that this day, this Saturday, would be the day. And here was the doctor telling my son that there could be no delay. It had to be now; it had to be fast.

After making calls all over the neighborhood and to everyone he could think of, all without getting anywhere at all so far as finding me was concerned, he called the doctor back to tell him.

Dr. Hughes, I guess, was pretty upset. Here he'd got this whole thing set up and now I couldn't be found and someone had to get the cornea, too. "Look," he told my son, "the cornea is all the way in New York and if we don't get it immediately and get ready for this operation, the chance may not come again for a long time. By the——"

My son, realizing that it might make the difference between my seeing or being blind the rest of my life, was desperate. He went out to make another search for me, and when I got home—and I still didn't know anything about all this—the doctor was on the phone telling me to get to the hospital immediately, while my son went in to the city to pick up the cornea.

"But you can't make it in time on your motorcycle," I told him. "The traffic is terrible and I don't want you to take any chances."

"I'll get a police escort, Mom," he said, and he did.

He was only nineteen, but he took charge like a real man, and he told me afterward about the ride to that New York hospital, with the sirens screaming and the traffic stopped, while with his escort he rode to the hospital, going to get sight for his mother.

That, he said, was what it meant to him.

At the hospital he got the cornea, all right, but what happened after that was absolutely unbelievable. I would never have believed it myself except that I know my son couldn't possibly have made up such a yarn. Whoever gave him the cornea put it into a heavy, insulated bag, and then said, "This won't last on any trip to Long Island unless you pack it in ice."

"Then pack it," my son said. "Do it right away, please."

But the attendant didn't seem to know where to get ice and my boy was new to a situation like that, and I guess it never occurred to him to ask one of the cops who were escorting him. He just took the little bag, hurried out of the hospital and across the street to a bar and grill.

"I've got to have some ice, please," he said.

"You mean, kid, you've got an eye in that bag?"

The man behind the bar took a look at this package my boy held. Then he said, "Son, I'll help you. I've got ice for you. We've got all the ice in the world."

Outside, with that precious cornea packed in ice, my son got on his motorcycle, picked up his escort and off they roared, this time to the hospital in Mineola. It must have been some ride. He had left the house in Hempstead at around six or six-thirty and he was back in Mineola by eight.

And at ten o'clock I was operated on.

That was the first operation. After that there had to be others, but it worked out finally the way I had always dreamed—I could see. Not perfectly, but better than I had ever seen in my life. For the first time I could see my son and daughter—really see them—when before they had always been only blurred, half-shaped shadows, no more. I saw my son, my tall, handsome, wonderful, motorcycle-riding son. It was so strange, going home after my bandages were removed. So strange and so beautiful. The children had decorated the whole place with flowers, the prettiest and the brightest colors they could find. My little granddaughter, a four-year-old doll, was there, of course, and we all had a steak dinner to celebrate.

Of course I don't know, nobody knows, how long these transplantings will last. After a time it will get more and more difficult for me to see and possibly I won't be able to go through another transplant operation. There's no way of telling.

It matters to me, of course, but not nearly so much as you might think. You see, I've had a wonderful opportunity; I have had these months of seeing, of being with the ones I love and seeing them, and the vision of them all will always be in my mind. If my vision fades again, or goes entirely, I will still have all these months to remember—to hold on to. That is the greatest gift of all.

15. Casualty of War

One of the most difficult realities to grasp in all of these lives is the variety of hurt and need, the variety of ability and disability. The sightless, like Irene, who may see again—but for how long?—is one example. In her case it was a cross she was born with, grew up with, has battled with, all her life.

War brings other kinds of hurts. The variety is infinite; it ranges from the devastation of the war fronts and bombs to the accidental dislocation of lives by separation, the wordless loss of one we love.

Working at the bench not far from Irene is a young girl who has been in America only eleven years. When World War II came in England Helene was just reaching young womanhood, and she was called up to "His Majesty's Service." With other young women she was assigned to mechanized farming projects.

Helene recalls how once a young man working with these auxiliary farm gangs, as they were called, got his hand caught in a thresher and was about to be pulled to his death. Helene held on to him and cried for help until finally the machine was stopped and he was saved. Remembering that moment, she told me, "Life and death seemed so close—and so far apart—to me in that instant. It was the first time I had come to grips with that reality, that close, that way."

Later, the bombings came, the Nazi "blitz." Helene lived unharmed through this hell-time in London. Her young husband, meanwhile, as a member of the airborne troops, had been shipped off to the Orient, to a forward base in the heat, sweat, malaria, and monsoon mud of the Asian jungles.

Then the word came from Asia: Her husband had been killed in action.

Helene and her mother lived together, sharing their tragedy and loneliness. One brother was a lawyer in England; another brother and two sisters had gone to America. Her mother missed these children so deeply that, immediately after the war, Helene brought her mother to the United States.

All the hurt inside Helene was for her loss, her grief. Through all the war and bombings she was unhurt physically. Yet in America, in a job in a supermarket, she suffered a severe slipped disc, was in the hospital for months, walked bent half way to the ground, went through a spinal operation and lived in seemingly ceaseless agony. For a time she was on drugs to ease the pain and nearly became addicted and had to halt—which she fortunately did in time.

It was then she heard about Abilities. She later told me that when she first came to Abilities and saw our people, "I realized how much more they had undergone than I, how much more most of them had endured and how much more courage and stamina it took them to win out, to find ways of leading successful lives.

"The first night after I started working," she went on, "I cried most of the night, not for myself and not really for them, but because what I had endured is so little compared to what they have known and lived through and conquered."

After much treatment, Helene now walks straight, although she still suffers. But she insists, "Oh, I still get pains but compared to these other people, and compared to what I used to have, I must not sound off with complaints. I'm happy with small pain. You have to be thankful to God for many things."

One whom she looks at with eyes of compassion is Murray, an expert cost estimator, who has worked his way up in skills and value to us in this job. Murray and Helene share a bond of the inner turmoil that each knew in the Second World War.

Each knew that war, and each paid an irrevocable price in it. Helene paid in the loss of one she loved, in the disruption of her life and her future.

Murray paid in even more immediate and personal terms.

When I first saw this big man, half reclining in his wheelchair-litter, talking with Ellen in the office, I had no idea who he was. The first thing I thought was: One of my eager-beaver associates is going to say, "We've got enough people lying down on the job. Don't give me this one on a litter."

So I took Ellen to one side and said, "Look, I think this is a very interesting fellow and I want to know what disposition is made of him."

I was afraid that some of our supervisors just might take the approach that we had enough problems without taking one so difficult. Even here, you have to keep reminding people of what they were and what we're in business for, that it's not enough for us to take only people with selected disabilities.

I introduced myself to him. "I think we can do something for you, if you really want to work."

He said, "There's nothing you could give me that I wouldn't try."

I didn't know his story then. I only knew this was a man fighting his way back to the world. It was years before I heard the story from Murray himself.

16. MURRAY: *Beachhead*

One instant of war I will remember. It was around three o'clock in the morning. We were in southern France. We were in our foxholes waiting to attack at 5:30. Suddenly I felt something hit me. I didn't pay much attention; I thought it was a piece of dirt or something sliding down my neck. A few minutes later, however, I started to get a cold sweat and chills, aches and pains. I began to feel myself to see what could be wrong and when I looked at my fingers they were all blood.

"You know, I'm hit," I said to the fellow beside me.

"Oh, you're crazy," he said.

He and I had been through a couple of campaigns together and had trained down in Naples for the landing in southern France and the push north. I'd been through plenty of stuff, especially at Anzio, where I saw a lot of guys killed and where I got nicked myself, but that was nothing, that wound at Anzio.

Sitting crouched there beside me in the dark he says, "Look, everything seems all right in here. You sure you're hit?"

I said, "Yes, I'm hit. Tell the next hole to contact the medics and tell them to come here."

And I started getting weaker and weaker.

Finally, the medics got there. They took a look at me and one says, "Can you walk?"

I said, "Gee, I don't know."

I remember getting out of the hole and I think I was hopping on one leg, my arms around the two medics, and this way they took me back to the aid station and put me on a cot and I asked them, "What is it? What happened to me? Did I get hit?"

The aid station was just a tent. About fifteen or twenty men were there, most of them badly shot up. There was a doctor and a couple of medics. The doctor examined me and they took my clothes and left me on the cot.

I kept asking what was wrong. Somebody said, "It was a tree burst. A shell burst right above you and you got yourself a shower of shrapnel."

I was thinking all kinds of things. It's your whole life running before you at a time like that. You are getting weaker with each second and you think about your wife back in America, the little baby you've never even seen, Anzio with its piles of dead, the house in Long Island, your job as a salesman, the big talker, the gladhander, ready with the jokes and smooth sayings. The crazy newsreel kept running over in my mind as they took me out of there, into an ambulance.

I was going somewhere, to a hospital. A big general hospital run by the Army, somewhere in France. All the way in the ambulance I lay on my stomach. I must have had a shot in the arm because I didn't feel any pain and I think I fell asleep. The next thing I remember is lying on a stretcher in the waiting room of the hospital. All around me other fellows, other wounded, men moaning and crying, men bandaged from the head all the way to the feet, and legs dangling, waiting to be operated on. I had never seen or heard anything like that waiting room. There were only four operating rooms and no space to handle all these wounded and dying men.

Somebody came to give me a shot in the arm, and said, "Boy, you're lucky. You could be dead."

That's all I recall until I woke up in a bed and discovered I was in a body cast from head to foot.

A doctor came into the room and a nurse handed him a piece of shrapnel they had taken out of me. He looked at it and looked at me and said, "Within a year's time, you ought to be good as new, but you may have a slight limp when you walk; your hip socket has been bruised."

"What else happened, Doctor?" I asked. "Give me all the bad news so I can stop worrying."

"The femur has a little fracture. The kneecap has been cracked a little bit. A few of your toes have been broken. I say within a year you'll be all right. We're going to fly you home."

I believed him. I told myself he wouldn't lie to me. I remember they took me to an airport somewhere in France. It was foggy and drizzling and no planes could take off for America and I waited, lying on a cot, and trying not to think and not to worry and not to doubt what any of these people had told me.

Yet two days later, still there, I woke up with pain and the medic took my temperature. They carried me out of the tent and into an ambulance that took me to another hospital. It wasn't really a hospital; it was a castle, a tremendous castle, a castle that was something out of a book.

This was a place where they had many amputee cases, pilots mostly. There were many casualties there. Men who must have been burned because their faces were all bandaged. Every kind you could have thought of—some you couldn't believe. And me, still encased in that body cast.

They said I'd suddenly shot up with a terribly high fever; but I guess I started getting better because after a few days the nurse said I was getting a transfer. The next thing I was in a plane flying over the Channel to England. The hospital there was beautiful. It must have been one of those privately owned places. My wife's brother was stationed nearby and he came to see me.

I was there several days before I began to think that my cast was getting bigger. Actually, it was just that I was getting thinner inside it. I also began getting infections. My right hip—the one that had been hit—began to rotate until the hip and the leg and foot turned all the way to the right and lay flat.

The truth was they couldn't do too much for me at that moment in the war. It was about the middle of December, 1944. The Battle of the Bulge had just begun, and a terrible flood of casualties began to pour back from the front lines and across the Channel. There just weren't enough people to care for everyone, and the newly wounded had to be looked after first.

I still kept remembering what that doctor had said. In a year's time. Everything would be all right, I thought. I was alive. I still had my limbs. That fact stuck in my mind. I'd be all right, I'd be walking because I had limbs. All these men around me, these poor guys, some of them had nothing. They were half men and I was whole. I should be grateful. I should be thanking God.

I stayed at that hospital in England only a short time. Then I was put on a Dutch ship and sent home. What a trip back! I was still in the cast and I was away below decks and it was late winter and the Atlantic weather was rough. They had to strap us in; they strapped me into the bed, cast and all, so I wouldn't be pitched out. That was a ride to remember, all right.

With our zigzagging antisubmarine tactics, it was St. Patrick's Day when we reached New York harbor. I was shipped to Camp Shanks, not far from the city. I'm about six feet tall and when I went into service I was a lean two hundred pounds in stocking feet, but when I got to Camp Shanks I was down to eighty-five pounds. I guess I was like a skeleton in that cast.

Before I went into service, my uncle gave me a watch that I had worn throughout the whole campaign, and I still had it on my wrist. When the camp notified my wife and family to come and see me, they went through the halls and the corridors, looking for me, but they didn't recognize me in the cast because of the position I was lying in, and the way the light fell, I didn't see them, either, down those long rows of beds. Finally my sister recognized the watch my uncle had given me, and from about ten feet away, I heard her voice, "Oh, I think that's Murray lying in the bed there."

I didn't know who was coming, and suddenly there was my wife and parents and sister, all there to see me for the first time since I was back.

It was almost incredible to see the people I loved. But everything was still mixed up and unreal to them—and to me—and there were tears shed, of course. It was a wonderful reunion with my family. But I guess the sight of me in that cast wasn't the most encouraging thing; they weren't used to the kind of things I'd been seeing and living through. They got excited, and talked with all the doctors, and asked what they could do, and the doctors told them not to worry, that I'd have only the best care.

This was only a way stop in my hospital travels. From Camp Shanks I was sent to a hospital in Ohio, where I had operations—it seemed as if every other day I had something—and treatment, intermixed with visits from my mother and father and my wife. It was too hard a trip for the baby I had never seen, and it wasn't easy for my wife, either, but she came. And wrote me all the time.

Once when my family was there one of the doctors told them, "We have done all we can for Murray medically. Now it's in the hands of God."

I didn't know that, and they didn't tell me. I knew only one thing—that I would win. Helpless and on that bed, I would win. Tied down here by doctors and nurses who had a hundred other problems and cases,

I would win. I would get out of this hospital. I would walk, now, tomorrow, next week, next year. When—who knew?

I was a prisoner of doctors, nurses, beds, and whatever it was that held me in paralysis of my lower limbs. This was the trap in which I was held.

I would not accept it as final; I would not surrender to it, I would not believe this was the final account rendered on my life. Over and over, I kept telling this to myself, "I will get out. Sooner or later—somehow—I will be back again. My life is not over. It can't be over. My life is not to lie here until I die."

After a year, I was sent back east to Halloran General Hospital on Staten Island. It was tricky to get me on a train on account of my cast; I had to be measured beforehand to make sure I'd go through the car window. But at Halloran the doctors started to take the cast off. In those days there wasn't an electric machine for this job, the way there is now. What they used was a pair of cutters. The hard part of the plaster is next to the skin, and the skin is sensitive. I don't know whether they gave me a couple of shots or not, but every time the interns yanked, I yelled. The nurse kept saying, "Good, yell. Go on, it's good for the lungs. Yell loud, louder!"

But when they got that cast off she looked at me and said, "My God! Look at this boy." And she called other doctors. "Take a look at this fellow's body."

I know I was a dreadful sight that day. There were sores all over my body, my legs were as thin as bedposts, my body was a blistered, bleeding skeleton. Yet somehow this terrible moment of half-existence was for me a kind of turning point, although they didn't know it, those nurses and doctors. It didn't matter to me how awful I looked; I felt that I would be able to fight back. My body ached all over from the sores. I lay there still and aching—and paralyzed, although I didn't fully realize that—but I felt, I knew, that I was free, not merely in my body but in my mind.

I knew it even when I heard her saying, "Doctor, my God! Look at this boy!"

They washed me up and X-rayed me. Then they put me into what is called an orthopedic striker bed about six feet long and a foot and a half wide. It's a kind of stretcher, with a compartment where you lie, a long narrow compartment. It has an opening where you can pass water. It is easier for the nurses to handle a patient like me in this kind of bed, because it has straps in it that they can fasten head and foot and a canvas that moves and turns you over, whichever way you want. You see, that way, they can turn you over every two hours, stomach, back, stomach, back. This helps to get rid of the festering bed sores and blisters, and makes it easier to put on dressings.

At Halloran also they performed one more operation. I still don't know how badly hurt I was—that some of the nerves in my body had been severed and I would never be able to move my legs again. I couldn't get a full picture from anyone. Perhaps none of them actually knew—or perhaps no one wanted to tell me how hopeless the whole thing was. I thought Halloran would wind it all up and I'd go home, I'd been in hospitals, by the time Halloran was ready to discharge me, two years. I was still in bed, I was still immobilized. But

I was still certain that I'd be all right; that I'd be out there playing ball.

One day at Halloran they wheeled me into the doctor's office—in the striker bed, you see—and he said, "Well, we're sending you to a fine place in the Bronx, not far from your home, a veterans' hospital because you're a vet—you're not in the Army any more, you've got a medical discharge. And you're going to this other hospital."

So instead of going home I went to Kingsbridge Veterans' Hospital in the Bronx.

I was at least a civilian. I wasn't a serial number any more. I was "mister" again, in the veterans' hospital. When you're still in the Army the regulations apply; everybody up, everybody awaken, everybody wash. At Kingsbridge, if I overslept it was all right. Wake up when you wake.

They brought in a lot of experts to examine me, to study the paralysis, to try to find out what kept my legs and the lower half of my body just frozen, motionless, helpless. And one doctor said, "Say, wait a minute. I had a fellow like that at a place where I was stationed during the war. Out in Ohio. We sent him home to die."

He looked at the X-rays and he asked, as if it just couldn't be true, "Is this a fellow named Murray something?"

The doctors at Kingsbridge said, "Yes, that's him."

"Oh, my God!" That doctor insisted on seeing me; he literally ran into the ward and when he saw me he looked like a man seeing a ghost. "Murray," he said, "we gave up, we gave up on you. We sent you back east—close to home—because we were sure you were going to die."

He called three of the doctors together around the striker bed and told them, "This man is a living ghost. You have to give him credit—he really fought for life. I want to take care of this case myself."

He examined me all over, as if I were an overgrown museum specimen. After he finished he told the doctors, "I want this man out of the striker bed, I want him in a regular bed, a three-crank bed for his back, his hips and his knees. And I want him down to the pool for physical therapy and I want——" He was like a general giving orders. In a matter of minutes I was in a real bed where I could stretch my arms and my back and everything. I was like a new person, right then. And I kept thinking, "Thank God, he found me, this doctor. Maybe it was meant that he would find me."

They began giving me treatments and training—and more operations. By now I had reached the point where I was pretty uncertain about whether I could ever walk again. I'd been in hospitals more than six years—I was four years at Kingsbridge before they started trying to get me up. My wife and I talked about it, and I told her, "Irene, I don't know what the outcome of it is going to be. I may be able to walk, I may not."

After all the operations, I learned that my hips were fused. They had fused by themselves, so that they could not move. My ankle bones also had fused. They could not move, either. I could just barely move most of my toes. I had just a little movement in my left foot, at the ankle, so they fused that too, by an operation. That was the safest, because I had to be one thing or the other. So it was—the other. My legs were completely fused, I was completely fused and immobile, from the hips down.

I would never walk. Not as other men would walk. But now they agreed with me—the time had come to try to bring me back to life. If I was paralyzed and immobile as marble itself, from the hips down, I was at least stabilized. Now we could attack the problem of getting me back into the swing of things. What they had to work with was a man—half frozen, half alive.

What they came up with was a tilt table. They could tilt the thing any way they wanted, up, down, sideways, any angle. They fastened me on to this tilt-top table face up and the first thing you know, they're lifting me, tilting me up.

For me, it's a ride to the moon. All of a sudden, after all these years on my back, the years in a cast, the stretchers and striker beds and crank bed, all of a sudden I'm standing straight up, fastened to that tilt-top. I felt like the biggest man in the world.

I was standing up, strapped to the tabletop. It felt good but there was also a lot of pain. This first time, my toes spouted blood, but that didn't happen again. They kept at it slowly, gradually, this standing up, a little bit each day. That went on for months, about eight months. Always, of course, I was strapped to this tilt-top table.

They got me a pair of shoes so I'd get the feel of something on my feet. They got me a pair of pants, the first I'd had in years. And they'd let me dangle my feet over the side of the bed. Even though the legs were stiff and fused, and the hips were stiff, I'd gradually get those feet to touch the floor, hanging by the buttocks on the edge of the bed.

After I started doing that for a time every day, they started putting me into the pool. They would put me on a stretcher and take me down a ramp into the pool. And I would just automatically float off the stretcher.

In the water, I could stand up. I couldn't move, from the hips down, but my feet would touch the bottom and I could stand. It felt good. It was exciting. It was an adventure.

The physical therapy was helpful. I began to get an appetite again. They would put me on a rolling stretcher and some of the boys would push me down to the canteen and we'd have ice cream sodas or frankfurters. I began to gain weight.

They tried me on the parallel bars. Because my hips were fused, I would swing backward instead of forward and the same thing happened when, about eight months later, I tried to use crutches. What I mean is, they put a pair of crutches under my arms but I didn't feel secure, the way I did between the bars. I felt as if I were on top of a building with a one-inch edge between me and pitching over the side, and every time I tried to swing myself through I always fell back. I couldn't control that.

The doctors told me that there was nothing more they could do for me. I'd been in hospitals a total of six years or more. And you might have said I was finished, that I'd be there all my life. But I wanted out of there, I wanted to be home, working, living with my wife, my child.

And one day it happened. The hospital people reached a decision. They said, "You've been in the hospital too long, Murray, you're going home."

"How?" I demanded. "How am I going to live when I get home?"

"We're making you a special medical bed," one doctor said. "We're recommending also that you get parallel bars for the home and use them for your exercises."

"You mean by this, you don't think I'll ever walk again—ever?"

I asked it slow. I wanted them to get the fact that I had to be told. The doctor said, "No, you won't walk, Murray. Ever."

Looking at them, I still did not give up hope. Fused hips and fused knees and fused ankles; they didn't stop me from believing. It could work out. It could be true that one day a way would be found.

One doctor said, "Look, Murray, let's be honest. At the moment, to reopen the hip joints would be a most painful experience and one with very little chance of success. I'd say about a thousand to one. Is that kind of remote chance worth it?"

So my wife got in touch with the Jewish War Veterans and we got ourselves a home. It wasn't too much of a home, it was a Quonset with a ramp so I could be wheeled, or wheel myself in and out. No stairs. And the people at Kingsbridge made me a special wheelchair-litter. It's just like a wheelchair except it has an extra platform to hold my legs straight because they won't bend. The day they put me in that wheelchair, they said, "O.K., Murray, go ahead. You're on your own."

Did I feel good then! After seven long years, after

who knows how many operations, each one more painful than the last, after never knowing if I'd ever get out, here I was, patched up as best they could, and going home.

I had a pension and disability insurance so my wife didn't have to work for a while and she and my baby and I lived there, in this Bronx Quonset hut that was our first home together since the war. That was 1952, the year you started Abilities.

Irene was wonderful. She helped me in every way, washing me, and helping me get on the parallel bars for my daily exercise. And being home, with people who were my own, and who loved me, this was tremendous. Because no matter how kind people are in the hospitals, they still are, to a degree, not a part of you. They're the world outside.

I had a cousin in Rockville Center, on Long Island, who sold us a building lot, and, using the GI Bill, we were able to finance building a home, a nice little ranch house for ourselves and our youngster—and the one on the way.

It was all pretty wonderful. But after a time, I realized something important: I was doing nothing. I was at home all day long. I was really getting in the way. I couldn't help my wife very much and I was just a useless man sitting around the house.

I had to get a job. So I got in touch with a fellow I knew in the Veterans' Administration and explained my case to him.

"Can you help me get something to do," I pleaded with him. "I can't stay in the house twenty-four hours a day. It's not living, it's not even existing. It's vegetating."

"Well, sure, Murray," he said, looking at me in my litter wheelchair. "But what can a guy like you do?"

"There's nothing wrong with my hands," I said. "I can do something with them."

So he said, "I'll see."

If anyone wanted an object lesson, I guess this was it. The VA man made the rounds for me, from plant to plant. He toured the highways of Long Island looking for a job for pal Murray.

There weren't any jobs. He would tell my story, how I'd fought my way back through eight years in hospitals and the answer: We haven't the facilities. We don't hire handicapped people. We haven't got the time.

Looking at it from their point of view, the gamble they thought they were taking, they were justified. If they'd known the facts, it might have been different. Many firms have learned that the so-called handicapped can bc a real asset to a company and can even lift its rate of production. But these people didn't know and didn't have time to learn. Even if they did, I was pretty badly disabled.

He came back and told me all that. Then he said, there was one more chance. "I heard about a place out in West Hempstead, a placc called Abilities."

So he told me about Abilities. And I listened and I said, "That's for me."

He looked at me in that wheelchair business and he said, "How are you going to get over?"

Well, I had learned how, with assistance, to get in and out of a car. So I said, "Don't you worry about that." My wife Irene and my brother-in-law took me to the plant and she waited while we went inside. I was on the litter and while Ellen was interviewing me, a man came over and looked at my application.

I didn't have any idea who this man was, but he shook my hand and asked a few questions, and he said, "I think maybe we can do something for this young man."

And Ellen told him, "I think so too, Mr. Viscardi."

That's how I knew this was you, Hank.

Ellen said, "Well, when can you come back? Friday?"

Oh, boy—Friday! "Good," I said. "Sure."

She looked at me as if to ask, "How did you figure to make it over here from Rockville Center?"

I said, "Don't worry. I'll be here, if I come by horse and wagon."

If you want to know the truth, I slid myself into the back of a cab with an assist from the driver.

First I worked on the bench, and in wiring. We tried several jobs until we got one that worked out best for my abilities—and also for the litter job. Then I got into cost estimating and I figure that's where I belong.

Everything in my whole life has changed since I landed that job. I guess I had been in limbo, a limbo of the living dead. And now I was back to life.

I was a human being. I was somebody. I wasn't just a human tree that once in a while had to be watered and pruned and fed. I was looked upon as a person, not just a wheelchair case, but a person who was out earning for himself and his family.

It gave my wife a little freedom, a little lift, knowing that I was busy and happy. She could do things, make calls, see people, go off with the children, without worrying and wondering about me.

There were the neighbors too. They had always been kind, but now it was different. I was a businessman. I was off to work in the morning in a taxi. And my children began telling their playmates on the street, "You know, my daddy's working. He helps make airplanes."

And where before they would not always know what to talk about to me, now it was all changed. Sometimes they'd see my picture in the local paper, and would come running in. "You're working for Abilities, making airplanes. What kind of people work there? What do you do? How many people do they have?"

It's one thing to be a fellow on a litter, sitting at home, doing nothing, feeling the pity of everybody and feeling sorry as hell for yourself.

It's something else again to be a hero to your kids, a hero to the neighborhood kids, as the fellow who was in the war and now makes planes at Abilities. One day we'll even make parts that go into rockets that'll take us to Venus or Mars.

It makes a man feel great.

17. Sergeant at Arms

The battle scars are many, and they can be found at Abilities, in the eyes and hands and skill of men and women who fight their way back to living, to productivity.

And there are some who have special stories, off-beat histories. Manuel is one of those. I did not even know Manuel, who was a comparative latecomer to our staff of nearly four hundred. He came to my attention abruptly, however, when I had word that Manuel wanted a three-day vacation.

Abilities is run on strict businesslike lines and three-day passes are no part of our routine. I objected to the idea and asked the reason. My paraplegic V.-P., Art, told me, "He wants to see his son graduate."

And then he began to outline the story. Later Manuel himself filled in some of the missing fragments.

It went all the way back to Quito, Ecuador, where Manuel was born in 1908, and where he grew up. As a youth he had seen some of the earliest planes flying overhead, and to him they spelled the future. When he was old enough, he went into the military service of his country, and in the 1920s, under a government exchange training program, came to the United States to learn to fly with the Army Air Force. He fell in love, as he put it, with the United States, the Air Force, and an Irish girl he met at an airfield in New Jersey. So he married the girl, stayed in America, and remained in the Air Force as a sergeant.

His travels, of course, took him and his wife and their children to many parts of America and the world.

In all these years of service, his love of America grew, and his prayer was that his boy would carry on in a military career, and perhaps even rise to greater things than he had achieved.

When the Second World War broke out, the American government wanted to give him a commission, but the Ecuadorian government wanted him as an expert in the development of forms and personnel and equipment-control techniques. So he served again—in his native Ecuador—during the war.

After that it was back to the United States that he loved so much. And some years later a large chunk of Manuel's big dream came true when his oldest son received a Presidential appointment to West Point.

The younger boy also received one a year or so later.

But my vice-president, Art, explained it this way, "You see, Hank, the older boy is being graduated day after tomorrow. This is the big week. His boy is going to be a West Point graduate and an officer in the United States Army and Manuel will have to salute him, you know. That's what makes him proud. Maybe one day the kid will be a general. . . ."

So Manuel got his pass to watch all the ceremonies at West Point, the massing of the colors, the bright plumes waving in the June morning sun, and his boy becoming an officer in the American armed forces.

And in a few years the younger boy intended to follow in the same path.

He is a proud man, this Sergeant Manuel.

During his own service he suffered a serious back injury, and it was as a result of this that he eventually wound up at Abilities. In most other plants, he would have the disability of age as well, but that is no bar at Abilities, any more than an amputated arm or leg is a bar.

In one sense Manuel stands as a symbol of the world-wide interest in the Abilities idea and ideals. For there are Abilities now in many other parts of the world; they operate independently but are patterned on our program. There is one in Mexico City and one in Paris, France and others starting in Australia and in other parts of the globe.

Disability knows no boundaries. It crosses all the borders of mankind.

In some parts of the world, the person born disabled is still considered marked by devils. But others have learned, as the world grows smaller, as understanding begins to spread.

One day I had some visitors at Abilities. There was a special Mass that day in the chapel and we attended. It was Christmastime. The choir—composed of youngsters brought in from a nearby school—was singing "Silent Night, Holy Night." All around were the people of Abilities, joining in—the crippled and blind, the heart-ridden, the diabetic. They came in wheelchairs, on crutches, on canes, limping, hobbling—perhaps a hundred persons out of our staff of workers.

The little chapel was crowded and the group spilled over into the factory space, where there were bins piled up with materials, wrappings for boxes, stuffing, parts for installations, and harness wirings.

As the music played, one of our old-timers leaned over and whispered to me, "What a strange thing to realize, Hank. This is a Roman Catholic Mass, and the organ music is being played by a Jew who has no hands."

I might add by a Jew who was born in Sussex, England, lived an extraordinarily international life, served in the British Army in Italy and Africa, composed serious music against the bombardment of the enemy, settled in the new-born nation of Israel and finally——

But let Ray tell his own story in his own words, as he told it to me.

18. RAY: *Tender Hands of Steel*

My people were Jews and I have followed and clung to their faith throughout my life.

If it seems an odd way to introduce myself, let me say that it is important, for this single fact has shaped much of my life, in an age and a milieu of violence that began with an overture of bombs.

I was born in the midst of war, in Sussex, England, and immediately thereafter my parents moved back to London. Jerry was coming over with his World War One variety of sudden death—hand-dropped bombs and grenades. I was in those raids, though I was too young to remember.

I was too young to know, either, that for me life was to be an odyssey that would take me from the desert to the hills and back again. from adventure to hell on earth—and back.

Dad was in manufacturing in England. In my earliest days, it was luggage. After World War I ended, he began making beautiful and extremely expensive gowns for the titled ladies of London. That was all right until depression came in the early thirties; then the ladies stopped paying their bills and my father was forced out of business. In 1936, leaving my mother and my sister safe in London, my father and I went to Africa—Rhodesia—trying to find jobs.

All my life I had thought of being a musician and composer. I had studied the piano from childhood. But depression is a realistic taskmaster; I had been taking extensive courses at the University of London in chemistry and chemical engineering, and for two years prior to going to Africa I had been working in a British chemical laboratory associated with a gasworks.

This experience and background got me work in a Rhodesian sugar refinery. My father landed a job in a wholesale concern. As soon as we were settled, we brought the rest of the family down from England.

We lived in Bulawayo, commercial capital of Southern Rhodesia, but at that time more like a frontier town out of a Western movie.

Then we moved to Salisbury, about three hundred miles away, where we stayed until the war broke out in 1939.

I was in the volunteer defense force set up in case of an uprising; everybody was in it, all the young men, and when war came we were sent into action. I was sent up to Egypt as part of the Colonial Army, shifted to the regular British Army, was put in the Royal Northumberland Fusiliers. One of our first jobs was to build dummy airfields in the desert, as phony targets for bombers.

After Italy came into the war, my unit was sent up to the border of Egypt and Libya. There were only a handful of British troops in Egypt at that time and I was one of them. We spent a good deal of time withdrawing until we were reinforced by other Allied units. Then we opened a big bombardment against Salum, which is right on the Libyan border, and took more Italian prisoners than we knew what to do with.

Fighting in the desert kept on for months. We could handle the Italians, who could hardly wait to get out from under the German heel. But supplies were short. The Egyptians were supposed to bring up supplies to the front lines, but they were undependable at best. Once, for a week, we were at the front without food, not even field rations, and practically no water. We were rationed to two pints a day; no shaving and no washing. You got the water in tea, one mug in the morning and one at night.

When I got a few days' leave I took a hurried trip to Palestine with a couple of my friends, to see and to visit the holy places of that blood-spattered land. This was my first view of the country which later became the new nation of Israel, and played such an important role in my life later on.

Back with my outfit, I fought all across the desert and up into Italy. There, for me, things got better, not worse. Unlike Murray, I didn't get hit, and Italy was for me the land of culture, of music. Music had always been an important part of my life. I'd played professionally. I'd even put together a band, back home in Rhodesia. I liked arranging and composing.

I had a big dream. I'd be a composer, have a big jazz band, write the hottest music east of Tin Pan Alley. A buddy of mine was interested in classical music. I used to listen and I'd tell him, "This classical stuff is easy. Mozart, Beethoven, anybody can write like that."

"Go ahead, Beethoven," he grinned. "Let's hear your sonata."

I took him up on it. In Italy, it's no problem writing music, getting a piano, getting people to sing. I tried it—the classical stuff—and some of it, I was startled to discover, seemed to go over. Even my buddy said so. And when we got to Florence, the Philharmonic Orchestra of that city played some of my compositions.

There in Italy, with the war nearing an end, another dream began to take shape. The Hitler evil was close to its finish. Some of us began to talk about a new land, a place where people could go to start over—people with broken bodies, broken minds, broken hearts, broken lives, a place where we could begin again, fresh and clean—in *Israel!*

Most of us were Jews in that little group, but not all. There were people from all over the world—the United States, Canada, England, Rhodesia, Australia, and South Africa. "The war won't last forever," we said. "Let's get together after the war, and see if we can't . . ."

The war was over, and I was back in Rhodesia, selling cars, playing the piano and trying to put together an orchestra, when a group of those same guys went out to Palestine. They found our spot for us in a beautiful part of Galilee, right under Mount Hermon, which was snow-covered the year round. It was beautiful, fertile land, just off the main road that ran through to Syria, to Damascus.

The rest of us in that little group were scattered all over the world, but we promised to join them. It was a year or two before I made it. By that time, the British had imposed a barrier on emigration to Palestine. You had to be devious to make it. In Rhodesia, I went to the passport office and who should be in charge but one of my old pals from the Army days. I told him, "I'm going to Palestine."

He said, "Oh, no. You're not!"

He knew I'd visited there and he knew my enthusiasm for it, but he refused to give me a visa. I had to go to South Africa and wait six months. Then I got one, not to Palestine, but to Iran and Iraq. Included was a transit visa that got me into Palestine.

My mother was dead by then and my sister was grown and off on her own. My father was a little sad about my going, but he didn't really object. He knew that I had to live my life, by my own lights.

And the light for me was eastward to Eden.

In Palestine, I joined my friends and found the place in Galilee as beautiful as they had said. There were at that time three or four huts, wooden buildings, subdivided into rooms, with porches on the outside and one big dining room where everyone ate. Several families and their children—eight babies, all of them under a year old, and a boy who was about seven—lived there.

This was a kibbutz, and a kind of temporary quarters, but a wonderful place to learn community living, government on the basic level, how to get on with people, how to share responsibility and work. On Saturday night we would have our board meeting, and talk about all the problems of running the place on a scientific basis: properly managed farming, where we could borrow extra funds, where we could get extra man power, how to use and budget what we had.

It was like learning how to live all over again. All who live there and work—not to work is a disgrace—are shareholders. If you decide it is not for you, and leave, you take nothing with you unless you are given enough to keep going awhile. But otherwise—nothing.

I had a good job in the kibbutz. Because of my mechanical-engineering experience, I was put in charge of all the machinery and the irrigation. We had a large area to irrigate and we pumped the water from a river about a mile away. As we required more machinery—tractors and balers and combines—they also became my responsibility.

At night, there was music and dancing, and I helped form a band for which I played the piano. It was fun. I was single, the girls were beautiful, it was an exhilarating, young man's world.

After a while, we began to get intimations of Arab hostility. Up to then, I hadn't seen very much of it, but one day we sent a youngster with some men in a mule-drawn wagon to another village and a couple of Arabs ambushed them. They killed one of the men and shot the other through the shoulder. The kid jumped out and ran back to the kibbutz. The mule went on to his destination—another village where he went regularly. The villagers all knew something was wrong when the mule came in pulling a wagon with no people.

We started to build defenses. I'd had experience in World War II with demolition and mines. In fact, one of my little jobs had been to go into places that we had just taken and de-booby-trap them. The Germans were clever with their booby-trapping. Some unsuspecting GI would flush a toilet—and the whole place would blow up. Well, I was back at the same old stand now, but for a different cause.

The Israeli army was still underground; the British were still there. At our kibbutz we had little antagonism against them. We all spoke English and when the Palestine police or the British Army people dropped in, we would entertain them as brothers. At the same time, in view of the growing tension, our kibbutz became a training ground where people from Tel Aviv and Haifa could come for a week and get instructions in military maneuvers, guerrilla tactics, and the use of firearms, right under the noses of the British. When they came to inspect or search for arms, we would take them into the dining room, serve them tea and crumpets, and they would forget about the inspections. Meanwhile, we would have the guns hidden in waterproof packages and lowered into the latrines. The British rarely made a thorough search. In fact, one time, when we were attacked by the Syrian army, the British came in with artillery and drove the Syrians out.

Incidentally, some of the land we had bought was in Lebanon, which is beautiful country. You don't see it until you go over a hill and then, suddenly, you find yourself looking down the long valley that goes into Lebanon. It is lovely, beautiful land, a beautiful country, but we had to farm this land with guns on our backs and with lookouts at every corner of every field.

Israel was in the process of birth, and the peoples of neighboring countries were assaulting the new-born child, and I was in the battle with the rest. I had been given a bus from Tel Aviv, a real city bus, and the only transportation available. I had a driver for it, and when I got our daily shipment of mines, I would go around to all the kibbutzim and Jewish communities of any kind and secretly the driver and I would lay the mines in a defensive belt around the community. They were all homemade—I believe they came from Haifa—but one kind of mine we made ourselves. It was called a "Duvidel"—a Little David. It didn't kill anybody. It just went off with a terrible noise and would scatter a patrol on the prowl.

My chief responsibility was mapping the fields, so that we'd be sure we knew where the mines were. I had a crew to put them in. Then I'd go around and insert the final fuses and cover the mines. This usually took me all morning. Then I'd go back to the kibbutz and put in eight hours working in the fields.

I did this for several weeks, even after my driver had been killed by a single bomb dropped from a plane—just a day after he had told me he led a charmed life.

We were using what we called "shoe-type" mines, copied from a German model. Each had a wooden box with an explosive charge and a metal grenade inside.

One day as I was putting in the fuse on the last of these, I had a feeling that something was wrong. The fuse was a little too short, it seemed to me. And my intuition was right. As I covered it, I must have put a fraction too much weight on it for suddenly, as I knelt on the ground, I was enveloped in a cloud of dust and there was a sudden whistling that kept on and on. For a moment I was motionless, there on the ground.

Then, slowly, the cloud began to clear and I looked down and saw that I had no hands. I was still kneeling and I could still hear nothing but the whistling and I looked down at my handless arms and I thought: "What the hell is happening here? What is happening to me? This is the end. This is the finish!" Then I began to feel a pain in my groin and realized I'd been hit there. That brought me to my senses. I was in the mine field—in the middle of it—and only I knew the way out. Nobody was going to come in to get me.

Well, I tried to press my rolled-up sleeves under my armpits at the pressure points to stop or slow the bleeding, but I needn't have bothered. The shock to the blood vessels had been so great and the temperature so high that the open wounds were cauterized and the bleeding was cut down to almost nothing.

I got up—my mind was clear in spite of my wounds—and picked my way carefully through the mine field. Then I started yelling for help. I couldn't hear myself yelling, and I couldn't see very far because my eyes were full of blood—there were hundreds of little shrapnel wounds in my face and all down my chest.

Funny, I realized even as I was yelling that my

glasses were gone. In most accidents such as mine, anyone who survives loses his hands and his eyes, but I had been wearing a special type of shatterproof sunglasses. They saved my sight, but they did blow off. Later I went back into the mine field and looked for them. I wanted to see in what condition they were. But I had no luck; they had disappeared.

As I stood at the edge of the mine field, all I wanted was for someone to hear me; to come and help me. My crew had finished, and I'd sent the men on ahead. I wasn't sure there was anyone within the sound of my voice. But someone heard—the "general," as we called him, in charge of our defenses. He reached me within a few minutes, got me into a truck and took me back to the kibbutz.

At that time we had a heliograph signal system and as soon as we reached home my friends began sending out a code message for help. Meantime they got me into our jeep and a girl who had been studying first aid tried to help me. She wanted to give me brandy but I knew I had an abdominal wound as well as the hands and that brandy is the worst thing to give anybody who is bleeding.

I told her that the best thing for shock is water but she wouldn't give me any and I had to fight off the brandy. I said, "Look, come on, give me some morphine." She was afraid—everybody was—but finally she produced the morphine and read the instructions. They said not to give more than one tablet, and to mix it in water. I said, "Come on, one tablet isn't going to be enough."

I was calm, but I was in pain, such as I never would

have believed anyone could endure. She gave me the morphine, reluctantly, and we started off to the hospital. It was a pretty rough ride. There was no road at all; it was all over rough terrain. A jeep from the hospital met us halfway. As hospitals go, this one wasn't much. It was strictly improvised and the staff consisted of one doctor and one orderly. The doctor was a refugee from Rumania. He didn't know Hebrew or English but we were able to talk in French.

"You know," he told me, "I have never had anything like this before."

I told him, "Save as much of me as you can until you can get me to a surgeon."

Taking those tiny fragments of steel, hundreds of tiny jagged bits, out of my body took them hours. All I can remember is the orderly's telling me to keep still. Then I must have passed out. Even with several operations they didn't get them all. There's still one in my side they failed to get.

I stayed there, because there was no place to go. The fighting was getting heavy and so were the casualties. Some were pretty horrible, especially the kids. A whole school-bus load was hit by a shell and a lot of little kids were left without arms or legs. I met some of them on my last trip back to Israel. Now they are grown men, with families of their own, working the ground.

I didn't realize during those first weeks that I had to a large extent lost my hearing. With more casualties there were more doctors and nurses in the hospital, and one day I thought I heard a nurse walking down the corridor. I kept hearing thc steps but they didn't seem to get closer. Then I realized they were my own heartbeats. Later, when I went down to Tel Aviv to consult a new team of doctors who had come in from South Africa, I went to a concert and even from a front-row seat I could hardly hear a thing. It was as if the music were miles away.

Not hearing did not matter so much. My hearing returned, gradually, over many months. But there I was —without hands. One doctor told me, "They're working on this kind of problem, in Europe, England, America. Read up on it; figure out who can do you the most good. Decide what you want, the way you want to live."

So I read everything I could find on doctors and surgeons and what they could do, and most of it looked pretty crude. There was one man who caught my imagination—his name was Kessler. In one of his books he described a technique called cineplasty that gives some movement to artificial extremities. This is a system by which articulating hooks can be manipulated by expansion and contraction of the muscles of the upper arms or sometimes the pectoral muscles of the chest.

I asked some of the doctors in Tel Aviv about this. They said, "Oh, Dr. Henry Kessler, sure. He's in the United States, at Walter Reed Hospital in Washington."

They wrote to him, described my case, and asked if it might be possible for me to come there. The word came back from some hospital official: Walter Reed is only for United States Army personnel. They could do nothing.

So that door slammed. But I found out that Kessler

had a private practice in the state of New Jersey. He would see me—if I could get to the United States. Getting out of Israel and into the United States became the next impossible challenge.

The red tape seemed impenetrable but finally, through several "sponsoring" organizations whose people were sympathetic and helpful, I succeeded in getting a visa for entry into the United States. Along with that I got my exit visa. I was free to see if this doctor in America could give me hands again, some kind of hands.

I was tired when I reached America late in 1948. Somebody had sent out information to the press about me. The reporters were banging on the hotel door. I was sick. My weight had fallen to only about a hundred pounds. I'd been five days en route by plane, with stopovers and delays.

By that time I had read enough so that I knew what might be done for me . . . and also that some surgeons take the shortest route. In Israel an English surgeon had looked at my arms and said, "We're going to cut you here, and here, revise this stump, and fit you with an arm."

I asked him, "What does the arm look like? What is it going to do?"

He said, "Oh, you leave that to me."

I said, "Oh, no. Just leave what I have where it is."

So now, in the hotel in New York, another surgeon dropped in. He looked me over and said, kindly, "How would you like a Kruckenberg? It would be very good for you. You've got a long enough stump."

Don't get me wrong. For some people the Kruckenberg operation is the best possible answer, because it does give some articulation; it divides the lower arm into two nerve-articulated segments which can be used as two somewhat awkward but serviceable segments of hand.

I said, "No, thank you. I don't think I'll go for that. What about cineplasty?"

Then he saw I knew something about it and he said, "Oh, Henry Kessler is a very good man for that. I'll get him down to our Hospital for Joint Diseases."

An appointment was made and at last I met Dr. Kessler. When you've heard so much about a man you wonder what he's really like, especially when your whole future life may depend upon him. And when I saw him I knew at once that this was a strong man, a wonderful man, and probably as self-willed as I am myself. We got into a hassle right away about what was to be done, because I was still thinking in terms of the human hand, and articulation of the nerves to five fingers.

This is a common attitude in all amputees, I learned. First of all they want something that looks like the missing limb. But then the big question, the really significant question, becomes: Is it functional? Is it serving its supposed purpose?

He knew what was in back of my mind, of course. I was a musician, a pianist. I played the organ. I was a man without hands and I wanted again to bring forth music with my fingers. But I was also saying to him, "How about control for every finger?"

"That's not a mechanical possibility," he answered.

"Surgically it's very difficult, too. It's very hard to isolate the muscles."

What he proposed for me was his cineplasty. I would have hands made of steel, articulated steel. Each hand would have what amounts to two steel fingers, each articulated through the actual muscles in the arms. "The hands are the hands of a robot," one of the patients at the Hospital for Joint Diseases put it. "But articulated by the muscles, mind—and soul—of a man."

I was hospitalized for many days. Because of the intricate processes involved, there were several operations. I was, however, allowed the run of the hospital because I was ambulatory with no need to stay in bed; two hours in the recovery room and I was up and ready to go. In fact I guess I was bothering a nurse named Lorraine; she was in another ward and we talked a lot but she kept saying that I was interfering with her duties. Well, Lorraine was awfully pretty.

Around Christmastime there were several weeks before I was to have more surgery so I was allowed to go back to the hotel. I was terribly lonely and thought I'd like to have a date with somebody. I had Lorraine's home phone number—she had written it on the cast of some fellow in the ward who had broken his leg and was getting phone numbers from all.

So I called up for a date. And that's how it started.

That first date was difficult. There were bandages on my legs where skin had been taken for grafting on my arms and those bandages needed attention that I, without hands, couldn't give them. I said, "You're a nurse. Can't you help me fix these bandages?"

The problem was how to do it without my having to take off my trousers. Lorraine finally said, "All right, I am a nurse. If you want those bandages fixed, take off those pants."

Which I did, and she fixed them, and then we went out to the movies.

The story had its happy ending, or I should say beginning, for it was a whole new life for me. As you know, I married Lorraine. And I met you, Hank, at J.O.B. in Bellevue, and did some of my beginning efforts in social rehabilitation as a kind of unofficial aide-de-camp to you. I worked also in New Haven in a rehabilitation center.

And I soon began again to learn how to use what I had left of my arms. First it was only the arm sections, really. Then it was arranged that I go down to Walter Reed, and a doctor there—they have the best prosthetists in the world, I think—made me conventional hooks.

The conventional arm prosthesis consists of a plastic socket fitted around the amputated stump. At the end of this socket is an artificial hand or split hook to which is attached one end of a flexible cable. The other end of the cable is connected to a shoulder harness. By simple movements of the arm or shoulder, the wearer can control the amount of tension on the cable and create a corresponding opening or closing of the "fingers" of the hook or hand.

With cineplasty, the control cable to the shoulder is eliminated. In my case, the power needed to open and close the hook or hand is supplied by some of the actual muscles that did the job before my hands were blown off. A specially designed set of hooks gives me a firmness and speed of control I would never have been able to attain with the regulation prosthesis.

I had never given up the hope of playing again. After the explosion, while I waited for several months in Haifa and Tel Aviv for the stumps to heal, I began experimenting. I got a couple of pencils, had someone tie them onto the stumps with strings, sat down at the piano and tried picking out tunes with the two pencils. I found it worked pretty well. You could, I realized, develop a kind of xylophone technique.

I even went a step further—I got hold of some Bach Two-part Inventions and found that they, too, went very well. And so I knew in my heart that it was not lost, that music and playing were not lost to me.

With the hooks, I had four fingers instead of two pencils, and I could play again. I think the first thing was a simple lullaby of Brahms's, and suddenly—with that melody—music was back. By attaching rubber tips to the hooks, I was able to devise a technique of piano playing which was acceptable professionally. I gave concerts, appeared on radio and TV, and was able to support my family while I was getting through college. My method of playing is like that used on a xylophone, with the hooks replacing the hammers. With my two "fingers" on each hand, four-part harmony is possible, and the pedal and an occasional elbow glissando add to the illusion of finger dexterity.

Later, with Lorraine, I went back to Israel and tried to help start a rehabilitation center, but that ran into trouble. In Israel there was too much red tape and bureaucracy and argumentation; those who need help will have to wait until the growing pains of a young democracy are over. There were endless debates and arguments about how to get things done. In the days of conflict, there were no arguments; we had to *do*. But now it is all different. I would have to wait, I was told after some months, for more funds to carry on. There were plenty of jobs. I could stay; I could earn enough to support my wife and family.

But I decided no. We would go back to the United States. Back to Abilities. We would start our life again, and rear our two children in our own home there, doing a job with Abilities and settling down in one place at last.

And this is precisely what we did. We found a house not far from the plant and my days are filled with an incredible variety of jobs, all the way from playing the organ at chapel to lecturing, writing, and helping to train new workers.

At night I go home to my wife and our two children, who take for granted the fact that their daddy is handless. (At home I do not usually wear my prostheses.) And my condition has given me, not pity, but considerable fame among the younger set. Kids I have never seen before in my life greet me politely by name almost every time I set foot anywhere within a two-mile radius of my house.

19. Music Makers

Whether the hands are of steel or flesh, even if they are only wooden pencils fastened with string, the music within will find its way to expression. It may be the handless Ray at our chapel organ, or Tubby in a night club in New Jersey, playing the piano, in his dazzling one-arm demonstration of the unquenchable human spirit.

Cripples, paraplegics, amputees?

Or people with music and laughter within them—and laughter is only another kind of music. Why should we forget to laugh, only because we have this disability or that? Why should we not be able to laugh, even at ourselves? Why is it so extraordinary that I should joke about changing my socks once a season, or complain to some overserious taxi driver that I sprained my ankle getting out of his cab?

Don't we all have to laugh at ourselves sometimes?

Do bald-headed men and flat-footed men and men with false teeth forget to laugh, to sing, to dance? I have no legs, but on my artificial ones I can outdance the average man, although admittedly there are some who couldn't learn to dance if they had Nijinsky for a private tutor.

We weep, sure, sometimes, like everybody else.

But we go to a party to have fun and to kid ourselves a little—and the world. Sometimes, at a big gathering, I'll be joking with some man, and someone will come along and give this fellow the word about me! "That guy's Hank Viscardi; he hasn't got any legs."

Right away—there's a change. Right away this man

who has been telling me an uproarious story, or listening to one of mine, grows solemn-faced. The weight of the world is now upon him. He regards me with new eyes.

I recall one incident when a fellow in a tuxedo, who had been full of bright sayings just one minute before, as he worked on his second martini, suddenly got the word and turned sad-eyed as an unpaid funeral director. The others hadn't noticed. I decided the moment had come to take the initiative in this kind of situation.

I began to tell a story about Johnny, my one-handed chauffeur, and me, one evening when Johnny made a U-turn—at my suggestion—in an area where unfortunately U-turns were not allowed. The truth was there were several signs up there that said they weren't allowed, but we just hadn't seen them.

Well, as Johnny completed the turn, this cop whistles us to a sudden stop, stalks over with that slow gait that presages trouble and says to Johnny, "What do you think you're doing there?"

He began to explain about the no-U-turn signs when he happened to see Johnny's one hand missing. "Oh," he says, "a one-armed driver, eh? Lemme see your license, buddy."

Johnny started to fumble for his license and finally realized that he was in serious trouble. "Look, officer," he said, "Not only do I have only one hand. I don't have my license with me either."

"You—got—no—license." This policeman was fit to be shipped away. He stood with his hands on his hips and for the first time looked in the back seat and saw me. "My boss—he has a license," Johnny said with sudden inspiration.

I said, "Sure, officer. I've got a license."

The officer leaned closer to me. He said, "Well, if you've got a license, what are you letting this guy with no hand drive for?"

"Officer," I explained patiently, "I do have a license but you see, I don't have any legs."

I thought he was going to throw a spasm. Johnny and I remained calm and quiet as this bewildered tower of authority looked from one of us to the other.

After a long and nerve-testing silence for all of us, he said, "Listen, you two, I would prefer to think that none of this is real. I want to forget the whole thing. I'm going to turn around and count ten and when I turn back I want you to be gone, understand? And if I ever see either of you again, I'll pull you both in for trying to confuse an officer of the law."

The way I figure it, we were half a mile away before he got to five.

The music of laughter, of song—of a band playing a melody in far-off India.

The story of Kurt is not a story of laughter but of music. Kurt and Ray are friends; their wives and they are a foursome, and it was through Ray that Kurt first heard of Abilities—and first applied for a job.

Like Ray, Kurt wandered the globe until he reached this curious new world called Abilities in Albertson, Long Island. But where Murray's story was of Anzio and a beachhead in France, and Ray's of the Sahara desert and the struggle of Israel, the story of Kurt, as he told it to me, was shaped out of medievalism and pageantry and ignorance that still, in many areas of the East, regards the maimed and crippled human being as it might a cur in the gutter.

Yet to me Kurt is also the symbol of a special kind of battle against the loneliness of the remote, of separation, of being away from the world we are used to, the world that is ours, of being in the hands of strangers, however kindly they may be, in a moment of urgency and critical need.

In some of his words I seemed to hear the echo of that loneliness, terrible and strange and impossible fully to communicate, that comes in some of the darker, emptier moments of silent, unseen, unguessed-at struggle.

20. KURT: *Maharajah*

By birth I am Viennese. My father was a violinist well known throughout Austria. He could handle most of the other instruments as well and also conduct. He had his own orchestra, a regular Monday night radio broadcast for years, and played at times as concertmaster at the Vienna Opera House. He was a part—our family was a part—of the musical tradition of Vienna.

Both my sisters played. My older sister was a violinist and my younger sister a pianist. I play the violin, the saxophone, and the clarinet. My mother did not play but she was a lover of music and our most important audience.

Ours was a pleasant and interesting life until 1934, when the Nazis came. While everyone was trying to get away, by good fortune my father had word from India that there was a post for him there.

My younger sister wanted to stay in Vienna, and my parents, who underestimated the situation in Europe, thought it would be safe enough for a sixteen-year-old. My older sister, who was about twenty-five, went to Italy. I was fourteen, and went along with my mother and dad to India.

The invitation came from a man who had known my father at the university in Austria, and who knew Dad's reputation as a musician. He had gone to India and was running hospitals in the state of Patiala. The old maharajah had just died; the young ruler was a lover of music. My father's friend knew we were Jewish, had read about Hitler's marching into Austria, and thought of this way to help. The new maharajah would get a fine new concertmaster and violinist; we would have our lives.

When we reached India I stayed in Bombay to go to school and Mother and Dad went to Patiala. Mother was terribly lonely there. She felt she was losing contact with her children. One daughter was in Austria, the other had gone to Italy, and I was in Bombay. So she made my father talk the maharajah into getting me a tutor so I could be with them.

A tutor was good for me, too. I couldn't speak much Hindustani—and it was a year before I mastered that—and the Indian outdoor squat-in-the-sand classrooms were strange to me. I much preferred being with my parents, and in our home.

But the big thing was the court. This good-looking, smooth-talking, music-loving maharajah held a regular court in his beautiful, dreamlike palace. We lived in one of the "compounds," which was actually a beautiful, walled-in park, inside of which there were palaces, not as big as the maharajah's, but big enough.

Patiala, of which he was the ruler, was run like a regular state, with police and courts and government officials and lawyers and taxes and council meetings—the whole business. My father's duties were special. The band was in a terrible rundown way; in fact it was a shambles. When it tried to play, the result was just about the most disastrous thing that could happen, even in India. The instruments were old. None of them was in tune with any other or, in fact, with anything. And there wasn't a real orchestra, just a brass band.

The maharajah wanted a string orchestra for his state, and that was why he had brought my father all the way from Vienna. My father was to build this orchestra out of the local musical talent. The Viennese Philharmonic in Indian dress.

I was about fifteen then and my father talked to me about it. It was a tremendous job. We had to begin to train an orchestra, as Dad put it, "from the cradle up."

We didn't go back quite that far, but we did recruit youngsters from school and they became the first musicians of the India string orchestra. I would explain to these boys—they were about my age—that this was a "government project." It was something in which they could take pride. So they began to learn the instruments, the violin, the cello, the bass viol—string instruments, mostly.

They started from scratch, these youths. They knew nothing about music at all. They would hold the violin and say, "What do I do now with this?"

And we would show them, my dad and I, how to hold it, how to make a sound with the bow, where and how to hold their fingers and their arms.

They knew nothing about Western music, or how to read notes, or time, or harmony. We had to start them in "kindergarten" and make them work their way up. And it was step by step; we had to find talented boys, bring them in, and set them to work studying and playing. I don't think anyone ever before built a string orchestra in that way. It was two years before they were ready to start playing. But they were finally ready and the first concert was scheduled. My father really worked on them that final week, and at last the big night came.

They played all kinds of music—Brahms, Bach, all the great composers, and also some lighter music. The maharajah just sat there smiling as he looked at his sixty-piece orchestra. He was very happy. He had brought something real and beautiful to his people—and to himself. He particularly liked to hear the *Song of India.* That was his favorite, I think. But he also enjoyed listening to a number called *J'Attendrai.* He had his lighter side, but he also liked overtures and some of the operatic selections.

I was—oh, seventeen, I guess, but my father appointed me concertmaster. We went to a lot of places and played a lot of concerts. The maharajah had many interests and he got the orchestra involved in all of them. He had tennis matches and cricket matches—and the orchestra played for them. He had Red Cross activities and charity events and the orchestra played at them. We gave concerts in Simla and Lahore and

New Delhi and raised tremendous amounts for the Red Cross.

All of this I found exciting, but of course I was a European and though I liked the ritual and the pomp and the ceremonies of the maharajah's court, I made few friends. The maharajah was friendly but aloof. I think he saw himself as a great leader of his people: he loved them; he would do for them. He was severe, merciful, kind and enlightened. Good-looking, he wore his uniform and costumes with great dignity; his wealth was limitless.

But I had only one or two personal friends. Most of the Indians were European haters. There was one fellow in the orchestra who came originally from Rangoon. When the Japanese took Rangoon, he fled to India. He was a violinist, and he had enough confidence in himself to make a 3,000-mile trip to see my father when my dad advertised in the paper for musicians. He didn't write—he packed up and came. He got a job in our orchestra and eventually won a scholarship to the Royal Academy of Music in England. Later he played with my uncle's orchestra in England. He was one good friend—a musician out of Rangoon, via India.

By the time I was nineteen I had completed my studies with my tutor and was working as concertmaster with my father, learning the ways of India, and various of its languages and dialects.

Then one day, as suddenly as a squall on the Indian ocean, I was taken with a strange illness.

I was visiting a place called Chail, the summer capital, about forty miles from the seat of the maharajah's government. I suddenly had a terrible pain in the small of my back. There were no doctors or hospitals there. I managed through a chemist to get a morphine shot. When that wore off I couldn't walk. I didn't seem to be paralyzed, but I couldn't walk.

Somebody got an ambulance to take me to Simla, where there was a hospital. But nobody knew what I had. The doctors got all their medical books out, to study symptoms and reactions. Polio wasn't very well known or understood in that district. It took weeks for them to diagnose my case, but finally, they said they thought it was polio.

I didn't know. I knew only that I couldn't walk. When I was well enough to be up, I found that my right leg was shorter than my left and I couldn't stand on it. If I got up on the toes of my left foot, I could stand, after a fashion. I made a crude high heel for my right foot and, with it on, I figured I'd be able to walk if I had crutches.

In that part of the world, no one even knew what crutches were. You were well or you died, so to speak. You crawled or you walked or you lay still on the earth.

My mother had died, there had been no word from my younger sister in Vienna, and from all reports the war was getting worse. Then this thing struck me and no one in our area knew what to do. I wanted to walk, I was trying to figure out a way, and even that no one understood. I called in a carpenter and Dad and I tried to explain to him what we meant by a crutch. We tried to tell him; we tried to draw pictures. It was no use.

We finally sent out for some wood and made the crutches ourselves, my father and I, and when I put them under my arms and walked across the veranda, what a moment of victory that was! It was like winning all the cricket matches from India to Eton and back.

Even with crutches, that year was the hardest. I knew so little about this thing that had hit me and there was so little information about it that I could get hold of, but everything I did read convinced me I was getting the wrong treatment for the kind of polio paralysis I had, in fact for any kind of paralysis.

While I had been in the hospital the doctors kept a cushion under my knees, with the result that I was twisted up like a pretzel, with contractions in my hips and my knees and ankles. I was being treated mostly by Indian doctors, although there was an English physician who made the rounds once in a while. The only good thing about that hospital stay was the room itself—it was private and quiet and the window faced on a wide green valley full of sunlight and shadows. To me, lying in that bed, it became a place to conjure up ancient gods and legends.

But when I left there after six months they had made no effort to help me walk; the servants carried me wherever I had to go. When I played in the orchestra, they carried me to the bandstand and placed me in my chair and handed me my violin.

They simply did not know what to do, how to treat polio. We literally had to figure out every step ourselves. But I didn't want more of this treatment. I wanted to walk. I wanted the best help we could get.

I wanted to go to the United States.

It wasn't easy in those days. A native of Austria was not welcome with open arms. Refugees had to prove themselves. The war was still on and most of the people we talked to said, "Everything is for the war; you can't get to America. Not now."

We kept trying. In the midst of this seemingly hopeless task, with everyone saying it was impossible, we had word that my sister—the one who had stayed in Austria—had died in a concentration camp. When I had last seen her, at sixteen, she had been so much a person, so alive, so fearless; thinking of her made me forget, for a time, my own problem.

My older sister, the one who had gone to Italy, had later gone to England, married a veteran of Dunkirk, and was now in the United States. So we launched a double-pronged attack, from my side and stateside. On our side, we had some powerful officials. The governor of the province of Punjab wrote to American officials, telling of the work I had done for the Red Cross. My brother-in-law went to the State Department to vouch for me, but wartime was wartime and he got nowhere. Then he wrote letters to the head of the Red Cross and even to President Roosevelt. I understand that many of those to whom they or we wrote, including President Roosevelt, saw our letters and were very touched. Whether this was why everything suddenly opened up, I don't know, but word arrived that we were getting transportation, by ship, to the United States. Not just I alone, but the two of us, my father and I.

And the day came when, from the deck of the ship, I saw the Statue of Libertv and New York City straight ahead. I stood on the deck on my crutches, with my father beside me, and I guess I felt as millions of other people have felt before: This was new, this was a beginning.

Six months and a number of operations later, I was able to navigate with braces and a cane, and most of the pretzel curves and muscle contractures had been straightened out.

I was disappointed not to be able to get a job as a musician, for this had been my life, but I did get work as a key-punch operator. And once I was earning a living I thought I ought to help other disabled people. With my violin I went out to a camp for disabled children near Nyack. It was there I met Ellie, who was also disabled, and right away when I saw her I knew she was the girl for me. We had a date the night I met her and not long after that we were married.

With a wife, I wanted to get a job with a future, something I could hold on to, but with braces—well, you know, the answer is always the same. Then, I heard about J.O.B. and through it I got out to Abilities, and all this world of people who have become my world, my people.

The *Song of India*, the band concerts, running to get the orchestra rounded up and down to the stand to play while the maharajah had a tennis match—all the beturbaned idiocy of that wonderful era of my life—all that is now only a memory.

But I did see the maharajah again.

A couple of years ago I saw in the paper that he had come to New York. I knew that he would be hard to reach, so I sent him a telegram.

Right away I got a letter back asking me to call his secretary and set up an appointment. But I found that his secretary was unreasonable. In fact I reached him three times before I got her! We made a date to meet just to talk over old times, and spent an hour together.

He brought out pictures of his children, and we talked about the green fields and valleys of that part of the world, of the band concerts we used to give, and of the future of India, a country that is only now beginning to stir and come alive. He asked about my father, and whether we had a band any more. I said no, all that was of the past.

Dad had returned to his native Vienna. He has a pension for his work in Austria before the war, and a pension from India for his work for the maharajah. And he has his dreams and his memories of Old Vienna, and the days when he was concertmaster at the Vienna Opera House—out of another age.

I write to Dad often about what goes on here, in my home and family, and at Abilities, and how training in music and my hands is helping me become an expert in one field of electronics. And I tell him, too, how my fellow workers and I get together our own orchestra, and once more I play the violin. . . .

21. Jet Age

Kurt is the story of adjustment. He has reshaped his life to fit his own circumstances, his need to support his family, the conditions of the environment in which he must do this. This is the kind of man we seek for Abilities. For we are a business, a going, competitive operation. The measure of our success is not in terms of a make-work program but in terms of quality, production, and price in the delightful, challenging, but no-quarter-asked jungle of today's efficiency-geared production.

There are exceptions, yes, because we are blazing new trails and all the values, all the techniques, of this new kind of operation have not fully evolved. Competitive as we must be and are, we are an industrial organization that puts its emphasis, not on automation, but on humanization.

Who could deny the traumatic situations that exist? They exist in every business in the world, but in ours above all. For the fiddle player who loses two fingers may be in a greater traumatic shock than another man who loses an arm.

This is the great secret of our operation—that each of us is unique in a more real sense than exists in any other business. And this perhaps is the hardest thing for the world outside to grasp, that the uniqueness of every human being, every human soul, in the universal sense, does not change because he has lost an arm or leg, or was born without sight or hearing, or with a twisted foot.

If we are to be Christlike to disabled people, we

must say to ourselves: "Here is a person. She may have difficulty in articulation. She may grimace and drool as with the spastic cerebral palsied, but there is a message coming from her mind which may be brilliant. Or it may not. But I should listen, at least. I must break down my own prejudice. I must accept her for what she is, a woman with something of importance, possibly brilliance, to say."

Until you learn not to cringe from disability, any disability, you cannot help the disabled. Cringing, turning away, or looking with eyes of sorrow—these are not the answer. We learn to laugh because laughter is a release from pent-up trauma. Ellen jokes about her difficulty getting into a car in a wheelchair and says, "Well, you don't have a problem with your skirts, and I do, getting into this blooming chair." Or I may roll up my trouser leg and say to the dog, "Have a bite."

But it is equally unrealistic to act as though nothing has happened to the individual, nothing is different. They—we—are different, in some respects. We face the difference and we make the adjustment, on the best possible terms.

I know a woman whose son was injured diving into a pool. He suffered a spinal lesion and became severely disabled. The family is rich and social. The boy could have been helped to make an adjustment if his mother had accepted the fact that there was permanent damage; that he would never be the same golf-club-swinging, country-clubbing, tennis-playing youth he had been. He could have made the adjustment, but she would not let him. She kept saying, "He will get better.

He will be the same as he was." The result is that he is on the road to chronic alcoholism. It is the only way he has been able to find an escape.

There is a difference. There is a need for understanding. There is the need to adjust and, underneath these needs, there is the wonderful ordinariness that binds us to all humanity. For, within, we have the same aspirations, the hopes and fears and loves, that all other people do. If, in the eyes of the world we live in, we could be the same as we are in the eyes of God—judged for what we are inside—this would be the greatest achievement for which any disabled person could hope.

There is need for solitude. There is this need in everyone, but particularly in those of us listed among the disabled. Some find their solitude in living alone, some in hours of communion in a church. I personally find it in prayer—and in the love of the sea.

I recall my first sight of a sloop, when as a boy—before I had any limbs—I went out with friends on the north shore of Long Island to Old Setauket. We rented a rowboat and went fishing for flounder. The fishing didn't mean too much to me but while I was out on the water for the first time, I discovered how quiet it could be. In one of those wonderful little coves past Northport and Centerport, I saw a boy and girl come by in a sloop. You know how still it can be in the fall of the year, with little wind, the water flat and nothing but the sound of the gulls to break the hush. This boy and girl glided by us, scarcely adding to the sound. I watched them and listened as the blocks and the tackle creaked when they came about and went on another tack. It was a fascinating movement, and I knew that I wanted a boat of my own.

Eventually I did get my own boat and found in the sea, in the solitude of man and boat and water and sky, a wonderful meaning that perhaps can be found nowhere else in the world. To be on a boat was to be away from the land and all the things that were on the land. To be on a boat was not to be different in any way. It was to be away from the stink of the land, and, in the days when pity and ridicule were part of my life, there was none found on board the boat. I still find it on occasion a very comforting refuge. The best part of a boat is just to sail it. If you have a port to make, fine; if not, just sail, lean back and listen to the sound of the boat and forget the sounds of the shore.

I suppose it may be true that there are sea people and mountain people. One man I think of when I think about the water and ships is Jim. He is one of the best men we have in the plant; in the field of mechanical and electronic gismos and gadgets, there simply is nothing he cannot do. In the plant some people kid him about the gismos he has on his wheelchair; I think it has three speeds, reverse gear and automatic transmission. We keep warning him he may need an ICC permit for interstate transportation.

Jim is one of the ocean-going people. He used to be a deep-sea diver. He knew the sea before he had any reason to seek it out for solitude or any other reason. He knew it because he loved it. For a man like this to be suddenly torn from it, to be told he could never again be a part of it—this is the individual traumatic experience. The fiddler and his fingers, the dancer and her legs, the deep-sea diver and his ability to plunge into the engulfing depths that hold—for him—the mystery and the answer.

For some there is no answer, except to fight and crawl and claw their way back to the sea.

Jim is such a man. A deep-sea diver, a skipper of his own boat, Jim has salt water in his veins. But the winds and tides of life sometimes drive us, with unexpected fury and disaster, onto the rocks. It was from such a moment that Jim's story begins.

22. JIM: *The Sand and the Winds*

During the war—World War II—when I worked on Army construction projects in Alaska, I learned that there was a big need for divers up there in the canned-salmon industry, deep-sea divers who'd go down for the salmon traps.

I liked to dive; I'd started back while I was studying at Ohio University. It was a challenge for me. I'm big and strong, I wasn't afraid of anything, and this was a challenge, going down into that darkness, fighting or fumbling my way through it to whatever I had to get.

So after the war I went back to the States, I and my wife and my diving gear—went back to Alaska and set up business. I knew people at the canneries and I managed to get a real prize—a contract with a packing company that was really a subsidiary of one of the big supermarket chains. Three months a year I did nothing but dive for their traps, picking them up, bringing them to the surface, and then resetting them.

We were a team, my wife and I, and we did this together. She would handle the boat and the topside gear while I was down below. When I wasn't working for the packing people, during the off season, I was taking on extra jobs—salvage dives and trap pick-ups.

This was ocean diving. In the southeastern part of Alaska, where the water is warmed by the Japan current, it averages fifty-five degrees the year round, and I used to dive in those waters winter and summer. I used regulation gear, and the truth is I was probably warmer below surface than most of the people topside.

There are different types of dives. The salmon traps are sixty-five feet to ninety feet deep, depending on the type of trap. In salvage diving, you go down to wherever there is something to pick up, whatever the depth. In commercial diving you don't usually go over a hundred feet. But you get careless. You don't feel the bends until hours after you're out, usually. That's why sandhoggers sometimes faint hours after they're off duty and why they wear a plaque saying to take them to a decompression chamber and not throw them in jail as drunk.

Then sometimes it happens that you get too engrossed in the job. That's what happened to me. It was in 1950—November 12—and I was diving for a wreck 160 feet in the water. I went down and attached some cables in preparation for raising it. When I came to the surface, one of the lines on the wreck snapped on the first pull and I went down again to do the job over.

This boat which was to end my diving days was a

real jinx. She had sunk once in California and been raised, and then had been brought up to Alaska, where she sank again. The fellow who owned her took her out to the fishing grounds, anchored for the night, and in the morning woke up to hear the sound of running water. When he discovered a full stream running into the boat, he jumped into his dinghy and got away just before she sank. Then he rowed a couple of miles in the open sea to a lighthouse.

But I wasn't thinking of that as I dived back down and refastened that broken line.

I had been back topside about fifteen minutes, and was having a cup of coffee from the galley when I experienced a sharp pain in my chest. I had an inkling right then what the trouble was, but I wasn't paralyzed and I yelled at the boy working for me to get me into my gear fast.

About a minute later, I was sitting on a stool pulling on my gear when I just went dead from the waist down. That was all. No pain. Just dead. I knew what it was; I knew what the bends were. The others on deck said, "Well, the only thing to do is put on your gear and get you back in the water."

In my gear they lifted me over the side. It was all they knew to do. As a matter of fact, it is about all you can do. In the Navy, or on any big construction job, they put you back in the decompression tank when you're injured this way, and build the pressure up to what it was before you came out, but we didn't have a decompression tank. A Coast Guard boat came alongside and they said, "Well, tell him to stay down in the water half an hour. That'll bring him out of it."

So I stayed down there, fifty-some feet below, for an hour and a half, waiting for life to come back into my lower limbs. Nothing happened. Feeling didn't come back. And it was getting dark topside, and dark there in the water.

So they hauled me out and took me to the hospital in Ketchikan, Alaska, which is just about six hundred and fifty miles from Seattle, Washington. There nobody knew what to do. They called the Navy Torpedo Station in Seattle and asked for advice and all those doctors could tell them was to give me plenty of oxygen and try to dissipate and get rid of the nitrogen. They said, "Get him down here to a hospital, that's our best advice."

I couldn't go by plane because the planes then didn't have pressurized cabins and there was a steamship strike on, so it was ten days before I got to Seattle. By then further decompression wouldn't help me. The doctors have told me since, that when I went numb like that, on the deck, that was it. That was when the blood vessel broke in my spinal cord and I was paralyzed.

The whole problem in diving is the nitrogen in your blood stream. All the gases in the air go into solution in your blood stream when you are under pressure, but the nitrogen wants to come out slowly, more slowly than the oxygen and other gases. That's why you should come up slowly. You stop every twenty-five feet and wait, giving the blood a chance to circulate, and you wait the longest at ten feet from the surface, to give the nitrogen a chance to dissipate. I didn't give it a chance that second dive, I came up fast and the nitrogen burst a blood vessel. It was as if you broke your back in a car accident, or somebody took a scissors and snipped that blood vessel like a piece of cord.

Actually, the spinal cord wasn't fully severed; there was still tissue there, and it was possible that one day, gradually, over weeks or months or years, it might come back. I didn't know, no one knew, no one could say, or they wouldn't. In the divers' union they had several cases of guys who recovered from the bends—caisson disease—after eighteen or twenty months, and so, I thought, well, I'll just sleep it off and one of these days I'll be back down there again.

They gave me the treatments, all the treatments. They gave me what the Navy calls "the soak." That's when you go into a decompression chamber for the maximum time allowable—thirty-six hours at a stretch. It's a long time to be in a decompression tank. They take you to different depths in the chamber—sixty feet, eighty, whatever it is—and keep you at each depth a long time. It wasn't too bad. They have medical attendants there all the time on shifts, and fellows in there playing chess with you—anything to keep you from going stir crazy.

My wife was with me in Seattle while I was getting these treatments, and part of the time she was just outside the chamber, watching through the glass and giving me encouragement.

Being skipper of my own boat, skipper of what is called a documented vessel, I was eligible for the Marine Hospital. Otherwise I couldn't have financed ten months in the hospital. I didn't have that kind of money.

After all the treatments—which didn't work out—I began getting rehabilitation treatment. The parallel bars, the learning to live with what you've got left, the works. Then they let me out. I was fairly ambulatory—with great difficulty I could maneuver with crutches and braces. I knew a lot about machinery and engines, all that. I didn't feel it would be hard to keep going.

But there were other things that I had to consider. There was my wife. I couldn't be a husband to her after this. She'd been ten months waiting for me, and I was no husband, and who knew how long it would be, if ever, before I could be a husband to her? She said none of that mattered; she told me again and again and she meant it, in her heart she wanted to mean it.

But I didn't want to bring her unhappiness and frustration. I was racked by what had happened to me, but I knew what was best for both of us—for me to set her free. It was simply too much to ask any woman to go through, and I wanted her, at least, to have a chance of happiness. We'd shared a lot—our home, the boat, and the work together. She was as much a part of the sea and the sands as I was.

I think she understood. People somehow do understand things like that, especially those who share the sea. It was all simple and clean cut; the grounds were incompatibility; we divided the property and parted friends. It made me feel a little more relaxed to know that she was not going to be burdened all her life with me. I could figure things out better alone.

Sometimes I thought: It's like being down there deep in the water. You wait and you seek and the darkness seems to close in but in a little while you start upward, and stage by stage you come closer to the surface, to the full light of the day.

I started toward the light by flying east to New York. I intended to go to Dr. Rusk's institute where they help the disabled learn to walk. But the night I arrived I developed trouble—a stone in my bladder that had to come out. I called the institute, was examined, and wound up at the Marine Hospital, on Staten Island. There I had a cystoscopy. There also I continued my rehabilitation work through that whole winter and spring. In June my nurse said, "Jim, you are ready to graduate."

There is a rehabilitation center on 23rd Street in New York and I was supposed to go there. But at the Staten Island Hospital I had run into a wonderful physician, Dr. Ward Schultz. We talked about the future and he said to me, speaking about the program at the center on 23rd Street, "Why don't you skip it? You've had plenty of rehabilitation already. When they get through with you, all they'll do is tell you to go out and get yourself a job."

I'd heard enough and seen enough to know the probabilities of breaking my neck on that hazard, so I listened hard when he said, "There's a fellow out on Long Island starting a place just for people who are disabled—a plant just for handicapped workers."

You never told me, Hank, but I heard later that what Dr. Schultz did was call up and say, "Mr. Viscardi, there is a fellow out here who is driving us all nuts. He wants to work in the worst possible way and somebody had better give him a job before we all go mad together."

Well, the answer purportedly came back, "Look, we have enough problems of our own. You keep him in your paddock."

And Dr. Schultz's answer to that was, "Thanks a lot. I'm driving him over there myself."

My interview at Abilities went fine except that there were two requirements. If I could get a place to live, and a car to get myself to work, I had myself a job.

I soft-soaped one of the nurses into lending me a car and got out to the island and before I was finished I had bought a car at the hospital and rented a room for myself in Mineola and I was in business.

I started in like everybody else, on the bench, as a harness and cable man and doing anything there was to do. Later, when somebody was needed to start making a few simple things, I pitched in. And as some of the men drifted off into places where they fitted in best, I succeeded in staying in what we call the methods or jigs department. I liked the work; I still like it.

But of course I missed all the other things—the free life, the job on the open sea. Deep inside, I still had a yearning.

You never know how things happen, or why they happen. At Abilities, I met Hazel. In many ways she was a lot worse off than I; she'd been a polio victim since she was eight, and not only her legs but her arms were affected. But she was working here and doing a good job and in talking we found we had much in common. Lots of things, but especially the sea, salt water and tides, the sand and the winds. So we tied up alongside, as they say.

Some people think its wrong for two disabled people to get married, and certainly it does have its problems, but on the other hand it has its advantages. Nobody's saying, "Let's go mountain climbing," or "Why don't we go dancing tonight?" or anything else like that. I helped her get a sling so she can go swimming a little and I go in the water myself, too.

I said to myself and to Hazel, "The sea's in us. We're getting a boat." We got a catamaran, which is a double-hulled craft that can't turn over and handles like an old lady at a barn dance. You have to have plenty of room to come about, but she'll do it, give her time. Hazel and I go out sailing on her, on the Great South Bay. One night I took a fellow out on the bay to show him the pleasures of moonlight sailing. Hazel didn't come along that time; just Johnny and I and a couple of dozen cans of beer.

Now the Great South Bay is no problem; anybody that's got presence of mind to stand up can't drown in the Great South Bay. But you know how people get worried. The wind was blowing pretty bad and there were reports of a hurricane on the way, but as I told Johnny, no hurricane would stand a chance in winds like that.

Johnny had heart trouble, and I was paralyzed, and we didn't sound like the strongest team in the world to put out on a catamaran on the Great South Bay in a hurricane. But we were pretty happy with the beer and nothing seemed too bad. But, unluckily, my outboard motor went out and with the difficulty of handling that catamaran in close quarters, I got blown onto the leeshore of a little island. There wasn't any way of getting off, not in those winds, so the only thing to do was sit there for the night.

I was sure Hazel wouldn't be too worried because she knew that I can handle the boat all right and that nothing could turn it over, but Johnny's wife got worried and called the police. They didn't help any when they called her back after a while and told her, "We've given up the search. There's no use."

But about six o'clock in the morning we heard the noise of a helicopter. It landed on the island and a couple of Coast Guard fellows got out. They came over to us and one said, "Well, let's get a move on." Johnny got up and they pointed to me and said, "What's the matter with him?"

Johnny explained that I'm paralyzed. So they said, "Oh, brother, what next?"

They picked me up by the arms and legs and hauled me over to the helicopter and flew me to my house, which actually was only about three blocks away. And Johnny called his wife and all was well.

A couple of hours later, I went out with some friends and we pulled the catamaran off the island and took her home. She was all right except that the sails were torn pretty bad. We didn't get them down as quick as we should have, you know.

But it was a nice trip.

23. Types

Of course, there are no types. There are those who laugh, and those who weep. But each is an individual case history: A boy named Frank, good-looking, full of all the young zest of a carefree, unattached and eligible bachelor. Stricken with polio in 1951, at the age of fifteen. Most of the time he travels in a wheelchair.

But Frank goes everywhere, like any other normal person. He drives a Ford and sticks his wheelchair in the back seat. He goes on hunting trips to Canada—one year he went with two other fellows in a Volkswagen. Three men and one wheelchair in a Volkswagen, plus guns, ammunition and hunting gear, is a real junket. Frank says it was great all the way.

Here is a bright, happy-go-lucky young fellow in a wheelchair. Does he want the pitying looks of his pals? In high school, the wheelchair became affectionately known by all his classmates as the "chaise lounge." In college, where he became a campus leader, it was called the "chariot."

"I don't have any trouble dating," Frank says, "except once in a while some girl may hesitate, then if she gets to know me, she'll go out with me and if I ask why she hesitated, I discover it was usually because she thought I might be sad, morose, looking for pity—things like that."

Last winter he went skiing. Of course, he actually didn't go on the ski runs himself. "I was willing to try, but I couldn't figure anything out," he told me. "But while all those guys were out breaking their necks on their skis, I sat around the lodge with a pack of beautiful girls who didn't come up there to go skiing either.

"What a time! Soft music on the record player, the snows and freezing temperature outside, the warmth and the fireplace inside, the lovely ladies, the hot toddies—well, I said to myself, if this is what they mean by single bliss, marriage will have to wait."

Not everybody has it that easy. I know another instance—a lovely young woman, also a polio victim. She was married to a prominent figure in the world of public affairs. When her illness came, something changed in the man.

She had been in the hospital a year and, like the other patients, was given weekend leaves to go home. The husbands of all but this woman came to take them home. "I could tell then," she said, "that something was wrong. And, it's awfully lonely when you wait, with nothing to wait for."

For this woman there was nothing, because her husband had picked this moment to break up their marriage. On top of her illness, there was divorce, and, because he was in government, there was interest in the divorce and stories in all the papers. All of this she went through.

I heard her story and was touched by it. I knew she wanted to work and was glad to give her a chance at Abilities. But the problems of her marriage, and of taking care of her son and herself, were too much and she had a breakdown. Then she came back to us, and I can tell you she is happier now than she has been in years. A new world and new hope and new viewpoints are opening up to her. Perhaps even new vistas.

Talking with her upon one occasion about herself—and life—I asked her what she would say to any young girl who might be disabled suddenly in an automobile accident, by multiple sclerosis, burns from a fire—any of a hundred things. "What would you say to her?" I asked.

She thought a long time. Then she said, "If I were talking to her, I think I would say—it's a shock. It's a shock you have to accept, but I don't think you ever learn to live with it. That's wrong. You learn to live all over again, and with it, but in a different way, and I think you come out a better person for it."

This is adjustment, revealed in words.

The truth is that we cannot run from ourselves, from our troubles, our disabilities.

This is one of the most important of all lessons to be learned in the struggle for adjustment, in the struggle to understand, to find answers for disability.

Handless or footless or legless, we run, in a spiritual and emotional sense, from the suddenness of reality that seems to overwhelm us. Sometimes we seek to escape from ourselves, sometimes from imaginary dangers, sometimes from ridicule, from domination by a relative, sometimes we run from an outer danger—the coiling grasp of some godless philosophy, for example.

There are such dangers loose in our world. Their victims have become, in fact, a strange new lost legion of people who have been mercilessly denounced by our enemies.

Janis is such a man. Personable, young, good-looking, with a special boyish kind of smile, and eagerness that belies his disability.

Like so many who went through so much in the

years of violence that snarled at young and aged, civilian and warrior, innocent and guilty, this youth was swept by tides he did not fully comprehend, seeking only a chance to live, only to find a moment of rest, of peace.

In the field of the disabled, we find—as here—the symbol of violence and terror, fear, loss, the loneliness fired across the world by the insensitive guns of modern tyrants. It is a terror that reaches each of us in some way. And each must find his own answers. The words of Janis are not fraught with emotion, but with action.

Behind the words as he related them is the story of one man who would not surrender to ruthless force, who fought it as he saw best, and fled before it, halfway across the world, as he sought one square yard of peace, freedom, hope—and the chance to live.

24. JANIS: *Flight*

I was born on a farm about ninety kilometers from Riga, in Latvia, the oldest of seven children, three boys and four girls. I went to the community school and worked on the farm, which was fifty hectares—about 125 acres—in size. All of us worked the fields. The summer, of course, was our busy time.

The house was white; the walls were of a mortar mixture built on the wooden frames to keep the moisture out. The roof was red tile. There were many rooms inside, six on the first floor and four upstairs. For a big family like ours, we needed lots of room. It was a wonderful world, a pleasant world.

We had a midsummer festival called Yanyudena. Everyone, young and old, would go in groups from one house to another, singing old-fashioned songs, dancing, drinking homemade beer, eating homemade cheese.

There were no speeches. Anyone who wanted to say something would express himself in song, in a simple kind of Latvian folk song. This is such an easy way of expressing oneself with a little experience that one can almost tell a story in verse, and the singing would go on for hours.

On Sundays we went to church. It was an hour's walk but mostly I went by horse and cart. It was a Lutheran church, and the minister was an outstanding man, a very important man to all the people where we lived.

As the oldest son, I had the special obligation to help my father take care of the farm. This is the custom in Latvia, and the oldest son does not forget. Mostly we produced milk and butter, dairy products. The horses pulled the plow in the spring, when we seeded, and the mowers that cut the hay. We raised most of our own food, and my mother did the cooking on a wood-burning stove. I still remember the smell of her bread as it came brown and crisp from the oven.

I was about twenty-two when World War II broke out. I was still working on the farm and was not married. I just didn't have time to think of marriage. Some of my brothers and sisters had gone off to school in other places. There were four of us at home with my parents when the war started. But before it actually began, when Austria was taken over by the Germans, I was called up for my two years' service in the Latvian army. I was sent to Riga, where I was put into communications—electrical wiring, telephones, learning electronics.

It was a good time. I met lots of girls and was not too far away from home, only two hours by train. I got home once in a while, to help on the farm. By the end of my time, all I wanted was to get out of the city. When you grow up on a farm, you miss the fields and the skies.

So I went back. But when the war came in 1940, the Red Army occupied Latvia, and everything was changed. Everybody who wanted to work a farm was promised a piece of land, and the farms all had to be divided up. Our farm was split up into three parts, but the people who got them hardly had time to get in their first crops when the Germans came in from the other side.

There was real fighting then, and for some time it was like living in the battlefields, day and night. The planes would come over and the bombs would fall, shells explode, and at night you would see the sky red with the glow of a burning farmhouse not far away.

When the Russians came in, we didn't see any brutality at first, although there were rumors that people had been arrested and shot. But gradually we began to see what they were doing and how much freedom we had lost. We could not disobey them; to disobey meant we would be arrested, would disappear, would be shipped to Siberia. Just as it was getting very bad the big fighting started, then the German troops came in.

At first the Germans were very kind. They pretended to be liberators, freeing us from the Russians, when they were only substituting themselves for the Reds. We were an occupied country and I was drafted—by the Germans—into what they called the Latvian Legion. In theory Latvians were in command, but actually the Germans were giving the orders.

I was a communications man in artillery, field artillery. After about six months' training, we went into action. We were told that we were fighting the Red troops, for a free Latvia, but of course we were fighting for the Germans and we had no choice about that; anyone who did not fight would have been shot down like a clay pigeon.

We were put into the battle against Red troops in the western part of Latvia. As the action began, the Red troops broke through our German lines. So we were in there fighting to drive back this wedge of the Russians, and we did. You fought or you died.

It was hard fighting, but the Red wedge was finally broken. The Russians were pushed back—not far, but back. I had come through the action with no scars.

But things happen when you least expect them. Moving from place to place I had lost some of the pins for my grenades. We were going across the fields when someone found a hidden stack of supplies, including these grenade pins, and I picked up a few. I wanted to be sure they fitted properly. I was just testing them but there was another fellow near me and I said, "I'm not too sure; you better step back." He moved back. I took the thing out and—that was it.

I didn't hear anything but some kind of whistling in my ears. Something must have happened, I thought. Then I realized my hands were too much shorter—they were cut off, cut off.

Blood was spurting out. I realized this was no joke, then suddenly I had a very sharp pain in my stomach and knew I couldn't stand very long. Somebody grabbed me under the arms and let me down to the ground. The pain in my stomach was almost unbearable by that time and I felt this was probably the end for me.

Somebody got a big jar of alcohol, not wood alcohol, but the kind you drink, and said "Drink, the pain will go." I drank a lot of it, and the pain seemed to disappear. I was only half conscious but I remember being put on a kind of cart, and then in some kind of automobile, and all of a sudden there was white all around. A surgeon and a couple of nurses were looking at me. They gave me something to put me to sleep and when I woke up I was all in bandages in a German military hospital somewhere. I couldn't move, I was in pain, and I was thirsty, but for three days they gave me no food or water; it was all intravenous feeding.

I realized I had lost my hands and that I was badly hurt in the stomach; worst of all I realized that I had only myself to blame.

The Germans were moving out the wounded and I was taken to the harbor of Ventspils in Latvia, where there were hundreds upon hundreds of wounded. Of them all, only four were Latvians, including me. We were put on a transport and taken to Danzig, which was also in the hands of the Germans. There I was put on a military train right away and after waiting forty-eight hours, went to Czechoslovakia.

I didn't know where my family was. I didn't know if they had word of my injuries. I didn't know what was happening to me, or where I was being taken. Surgeons had already operated on various parts of my body to remove shell fragments. But what was to come next?

For a time I was in a hospital in a place called Hirschberg. The war fronts moved fast. We would stay in one place until it became too "hot." Then we would be moved to another hospital. Four days in one hospital, two months in another, three weeks in a third, five weeks in a fourth.

I had a few letters from home. My family had found out what had happened from some of the others in my unit. But I did not hear from the farm; with the trouble and the war, the family was split up. Some were in the western part of Latvia, still under the Nazis; my father was in the eastern part under the Reds. There was no word at all from him.

In Bavaria a doctor operated on my eye to remove a fragment. Then I was back in Czechoslovakia, always in hospitals. But my wounds were healing. My arms were covered with flesh and new skin. The war was coming to an end and the Allies were closing in on the German territory from all sides.

I was in Prague when we learned that the American army was arriving. I thought that would be good. I would stay there and wait for the Americans. But suddenly the Americans pulled back and the Reds advanced and I realized that I could not stay there, unless I wanted to be "liberated" again by the Communists. I was still not fully recovered, but I could walk pretty well and I decided to try to get out of Czechoslovakia any way I could, into Bavaria. Everything then was in a state of chaos.

The German authorities said, "Everyone who can walk, will walk." And we did. We had very little with us to carry, and sometimes we could get a ride on a truck for ten or fifteen kilometers, but mostly we walked. I got into a group of civilians, perhaps fifty or sixty men, women, and children, all going along the road together. We all helped one another. I was the only one really disabled, but some of the old people were ill, and couldn't walk as well or as long as I could.

We came to the Erzgebirge Mountains, the old people and me and the children and all the others, and up we went.

At night we would stop wherever we could find a stove and would cook up some food, anything, to keep us alive and warm. Some of the people got so terribly weak that we could make only three or four miles a day. My shoes began to fall off and someone gave me another pair. And in my new shoes on I went with the rest, running from the Russians.

It was spring. The hills were beautiful. Nature was peaceful. It was hard to believe that here we were, a little band running for our lives—or for our freedom.

At last we were at the border between Czechoslovakia and Bavaria, at the Eger River. On the other side were American forces. We were that close to freedom—to escape. And the word kept coming, the Russians are closing in, the Russians have taken this, the Russians are coming here.

The bridges across the river were guarded and the gates were down. You could go across only when they allowed you to. We talked with the American guards and they questioned us and I guess they realized what the situation was, and why we wanted so much to get to the other side of that river. Finally they said, "All right. This group of refugees can cross the bridge."

So the gates were opened and we went across to the

other side. What a great rush of relief to know we were safe.

There were all kinds of people and American officers asking us questions. They had set up camps for refugees and displaced persons and there was food, and lodging, and medical care. The military officials began sorting us out, sending us to different places. I arrived after a short trip on a truck at a camp where there were all types of people, speaking every kind of language.

There were literally thousands of displaced persons in that camp. Right then there were millions of people all over Germany—Poles and Russians, Estonians, Latvians, and Czechs, people of every nation and locality—and the Americans were trying to sift them out. I was with people from the Baltic countries and we worked in kitchens while they made plans to send us back.

I didn't want to go back and live under the Reds; I had tasted that in 1940. I had seen how anyone who raised his voice was arrested and sent to Siberia. I had seen eighteen people in my own community disappear. Of course, people disappeared, too, when the Germans came in, especially the Jews.

But whatever happened, without hands I would be no use any more on the farm. I was glad I was in the American zone. But there were complications; authorities were sending everybody back, or trying to. Russians went back to Russia, Poles to Poland. But we said, some of us there, "No, we don't want to go back. We are afraid."

The American officials said, "You have to go back."

I said, "No—please. I won't go back."

"All right," they said, "we will talk it over." The

big problem was that I was in uniform. Civilians were given different treatment. I realized then that maybe the only way I could avoid being sent back was to forget I was in the army, so by self-proclamation I became a civilian again. Well, it all straightened itself out and I was not forced to go back. Thousands, tens of thousands, of others had to go back because they had been in the Russian or German armed forces, and it must have been hell for them. I think, because of my accident, because I had no hands, the displaced-persons officials gave me an extra chance.

The world was upside down; there was no time—you lost track of time. This camp for a month; then another in the Alps in Italy, for four, five months. From there to a refugee camp. Every two months or so we would be called in for questions, for screening. Who are you? What are you? Why?

I went into a third camp in Upper Bavaria, a beautiful camp where I had an operation on my stumps, and later, in another camp near Salzburg, I had a Kruckenberg operation on one arm, which gave me some articulation at the end of the stump.

After a while I had word from my family. They were all still alive, but with the end of the war the cattle were all destroyed on the farm, and there was no food, no milk, nothing, and the occupation was severe. My father and mother and sisters—everybody still on the farm—was shipped to Siberia because they had not fought for the Russians and because they believed that Latvia should be a free country. And that lasted, that exile, for eight years.

By the time they came back, Stalin was dead and

things in Russia itself had changed. My father was close to eighty when he got back. My mother was sick, dying from cancer, but she saw her own land once more before she died.

My younger sister had grown up in Siberia, really, and when she came back she went to a Russian high school, met a Russian boy whom she married, and they went back to Siberia together, voluntarily, to work and live.

One of my brothers is working in Latvia as an electrician, and two sisters are there too; one is a nurse and the other supervises a kindergarten. They are happy with the way things are. But there is no one from our family on the farm now; it is in other hands.

While I was in the Salzburg refugee camp, I was still nursing the big dream of getting to the United States. I kept myself busy. I taught myself to eat properly, to feed myself. I did whatever I could to learn about the United States. Then I was switched to a camp on the Danube, at Neuberg, where there were many disabled people.

I kept saying to myself, if I could get through the screenings, the political screenings and the physical examinations, and get to America, what a wonderful thing that would be. I dreamed of having a chance to experience what it was like in America.

Then the word came. The authorities had checked on my story, my background, on my brother, who, I learned, had gone into the American army. I could go to America.

So I came to the free world. What I saw was different

from anything I had seen in all my wanderings, all my flight. It was not just the great buildings of Manhattan, the bridges, the lights; it was much more because it was the people, all the mixtures of the world. Only here, despite troubles and quarrels and difficulties on occasion, here they lived in peace.

And here I met many who wanted to help me, and out of this was given—through Dr. Howard Rusk and Mrs. Eleanor Roosevelt—an introduction to Abilities, and a chance to start with a job in America.

When I first came to the United States, I thought I would stay only perhaps two years and then go back to Europe. But now I know this is my home, this is where I will stay, hands or no hands. I made one trip back to Germany to see my two brothers and I returned to the United States. I know that I will miss my family, I will miss the farm, some of the old customs, the singing and dancing of a summer festival night.

But the world doesn't stand still and the past is long dead. I think about the future and possible marriage and a home and family of my own.

Somewhere on Long Island, I imagine.

25. Odyssey

From Latvia, Vienna, Alaska, South Africa. From California, Ohio, Brooklyn, the Bronx.

They have a saying about this at Abilities: If you let them help you build a better mousetrap, the disabled will beat a path to your door from all over the world.

They do. They come, they call, they write.

Sometimes the letters are moving. Sometimes they come, not from would-be workers, but from people who have merely heard about us, or read some article or book. One letter came from a little girl in Holmesville, Ohio:

> Dear Mr. Viscardi:
>
> I have read the story of your life. I know how you felt. I am crippled too. But my feet can be saved. I can use my feet but I was born with a form of clubbed feet. I have to walk up on the toes of my left foot and my right foot is getting that way, too.
>
> I know how hard it was to walk. I have a terrible time walking. . . .
>
> I am fifteen now. I hated every morning when my mother would call me for school. I felt I was going through a day of nothing but hate for me.
>
> Everybody seemed to notice my feet. . . . I was just about ready to call it quits when I went to a bone specialist and he said an operation would clear it up good as new.

So I am going for my operation October 3. I am being operated on the 4th.

Sincerely yours,
Lucy

And Lucy did have her operation and her feet are as good as new, according to the answer I received to my letter. And this makes us happy for a fifteen-year-old girl from Ohio.

By letter, by phone or in person. Sometimes the story of these odysseys varies from the ordinary run. In the case of Hal it was a special interest in a special world, the carnivals.

Carnivals, like the circus, have an appeal to all who have wanderlust and a yearning for adventure, even those who may have to do their wandering in a wheelchair. Hal belonged to this select group.

The story of Hal might appear to be one of restlessness. But to understand we must recognize his disability and his unwillingness to let it hinder him, in the quest for the magic moments of life, for excitement, for adventure, for the far-off laughter.

Big, bluff, full of the need to taste the world, Hal followed a path far different than many of those who came to Abilities—indeed different from most of those who sit in wheelchairs all their lives. He was guided by a courage in his heart—an unfettered, casual, offhand courage he hardly recognizes himself.

This is perhaps the heart of his story, this willingness to seek out the most rugged type of adventure—wheelchair, braces and all. The ruggedness of the world into which Hal moved he accepted on its own terms. The rains, the storms, the winds, the near disasters, the whole precarious state—and the uncertain panoply of stars above the carnival world.

And when it was over, when he decided to pull up stakes, he headed for——but that is his story, his report—or should I say his spiel?—as Hal told it to me.

26. HAL: *Carnival*

I got into the world of carnival originally through my sister. But not before I was in a wheelchair. I was hit with infantile when I was only eighteen months old, but I always walked pretty well and it wasn't until I was twenty-seven that things got so rugged walking that I decided: "It's the chair for me, brother, and save the gams."

Before that I was a jewelry maker. I'd taken courses at the Institute for the Crippled and Disabled down on 23rd Street in New York. I learned to make jewelry, costume jewelry, and I'd go all over town selling the stuff to the stores. Then I started having a problem. I'd fall down. My legs would just give in under me. Just like that. Well, I knew what was going. I had to go out and get myself a wheelchair.

Jewelry factories are small and you can't get around

in them in a wheelchair, so I had to find another line for myself. One of my sisters was in the carnival business and I said to myself, "Being that you are in a wheelchair, why don't you take a fling at the carnival business?" I was going for a lark in any case.

My sister and her husband got into the carney business through a fellow they met when they were running a restaurant in Miami, and talking to them I'd found that a carnival is a special place where all the world's equal. You've got one leg or two or none, it doesn't matter. Can you do a job? Can you bring the people in? Can you rake in the quarters and half dollars? That's all.

I was living on the East Side of Manhattan in a building where I had to walk up one flight, and either my sister or her husband or my nephew, whoever was there, had to pull me up those stairs. They didn't mind, but I did. When this sister came back from a road trip, hopscotching with the carnival, going where the money was, she would tell me all the exciting things that had happened and to me it sounded like a ball.

I suppose it was the way somebody else might think about a trip to Europe, or a safari to Africa, or a junket to see the ruins of Greece or Egypt. Everybody has a secret place he wants to get to, once. A place that spells adventure to him, and it doesn't matter if you can walk or not, or swim, or go in a rocket. It's the idea of finding this one thing, taking this trip, climbing this giant of a mountain. That's the way it was with me, listening to her.

So now that I couldn't walk at all, now that the

chair had become feet and legs for me, I knew I wanted to go the carnival road.

So they said to me, "O.K., Hal, you want to do it—you ought to. We'll go along. We'll talk to O.C., the owner. We'll fix it up so you can talk with him. Then you're on your own."

Well I got the job.

It turned out I had a couple of chores with the carnival. One was to do palm reading. That's a good clean operation. And then I worked one of the games. During the matinees, I used to have a grab bag I sold to the kiddies, always something inside, a gift for every youngster, a prize in every bag. You know the lingo. And I worked a ball game—you rolled a ping-pong ball down a little incline and whatever number you hit, that was what you won, see?

In the carnival business, a disabled person means nothing. He's just one of the guys. I guess they're so used to seeing crazy-looking people in the Ten-in-One shows—that's the side show, the freak show—that they accept them just as people. They just treat you like everybody else. They didn't make any exceptions. You just follow along in the mud with the wheelchair up to the hub in mire. But it was all right. It was excitement—the crowds, the people, the language, the whole thing, the way I'd always dreamed it.

Of course, let's face it, traveling like that wasn't the easiest, and the profits weren't the greatest, and the future, you might say, wasn't the rosiest. So where was I going with my wheelchair and my paralysis and my life? I didn't want to do what we call "home work"—

jobs at home, you know. I'd done that before, and what did I make? Enough to buy myself a package of cigarettes. I had to have better than that.

Well, I was back in New York and my sister and her girl friend and I all applied for jobs and I was told I'd have to get a statement from my doctor that I was physically able to work before I could be considered. I was going to get the statement when my sister's friend began to tell me she had read about a place called Abilities. I said, "All right, let's go."

So over we went. That was right at the start, when the whole Abilities setup was still in the garage in West Hempstead, and the organization wasn't nearly the size it was to become later. I went in and was interviewed and a week later got a call and came in and went to work. Of course, I'd worked on machines in the jewelry business so I was used to delicate work like that and it was no problem to pick up any of the jobs on the bench.

While I was working for you, Hank, I was also remembering carney days and thinking about those tents they lug around from city to city. They all the time take 'em down and put 'em up, and there must be at least a hundred and fifty pieces, maybe more, all numbered, and each one has to go in the right place. During the tearing down and putting up, people hate each other. Even marriages have been known to go on the rocks when a piece was lost.

I figured out a way to make the whole tent frame out of aluminum, in three pieces, and all you had to do was put them together and throw the canvas over them. I worked on this in my spare time and finally I decided it was a big deal and I ought to give it a whirl. That was when I came to the front office and said, "This carnival business, Hank, is in my blood and I've got this tent idea. Maybe it's good, maybe not. I want to give it a try."

So I rounded up a couple of pals and we got ourselves into a carnival. We had one sample tent and when we started putting it up everybody crowded around us and asked, "What have you got there?"

I said, "It's a tent. We're putting it up in ten minutes."

Well, sure enough, it was up in ten minutes. Then they all began asking where they could get one and how much it cost and we began taking orders. Our problem was, where could we make all these things? Finding a place and finding the initial capital—capital wasn't easy, we found out.

The first one we made in my own back yard, three of us, but then one of the fellows left, and I couldn't make them alone or even with one man working with me, and we didn't have the funds to hire the help we needed. A story got into one of the business papers and then I got swamped with orders—but the cash wasn't there. I've got the patent on it. But I have had to hold up. One day, maybe. . . .

But anyway, I had my try, and stayed with the show, after we gave up on the tent. I had a dart game—throw the dart, win a prize. I even had fruit—win yourself a grapefruit. The last one I used was the simplest and the best—three old-fashioned milk cans and three indoor baseballs. You throw the three baseballs into any single can and you win a prize.

This was a big show and traveled in cars, about seventy-five cars there were. Four Ferris wheels, a big scooter, three girlie shows, about nine other shows, the Ten-in-One show, the animal show, and the midget show.

The people in the carney are like out of a story. One fellow didn't have any legs and only one arm. He was born that way. He did an act and also tattooing. And another fellow had no legs—he had lost them in an accident, driving midget racers—and he did an act with no legs in the motordrome, riding a motorcycle real fast around the drome, with no legs.

There's a life in the carnival the world outside never sees, like the geeks. A geek is a fellow who'll do anything for a drink. I mean, he'll play patsy to a pitchman, he'll do crazy stunts, he can be the biggest drawing card you've got, but lots of carnivals don't like to use them; we didn't. We had one who hung around. One day everybody thought he was dead. He was lying there motionless as death itself and nothing could get him up. But it was just the old bottle and it wore off.

There's the roughies—the men who put up the tent. They're the toughest men in the world. They're drifters—in for a day or two, and gone. Sleep wherever they happen to be. You'll find 'em behind a tent, in the middle of the Midway, who knows? They can outfight, outswear, outlift, and in general outdo everybody around the show.

And the carnival wife. When you get a carney wife, why, you just make friends. She's your wife for maybe a season. So long as you give her room and board, she's your wife. That's the way they live—not the way I live or believe, you understand. But she's your wife, she'll help you in whatever concession you've got, she'll be right there. And next season—who knows?

The carnival is one great pitch, you could say. It's everything in life that's good, bad, or indifferent. It's people at their best and worst, life at its best and worst. This is why I had to try it and why I had to run back to it and try that tent pitch.

I've done about everything in the carnival; I know about it. I've been a talker on the show, on all of them, the girlie shows included. Your voice goes out on the PA system and the crowds come up around you to listen. You pick up the words without any trouble. *Come on in and see the girls. They're doing it now. Come on in, plenty of seats for everybody. Now watch her, look at her, she's a nice little thing. She shakes like a bowl of jelly on a frosty morning, my gosh. Look at her. Say, if you're over sixty you can't stand it, and if you're under sixty, you can't understand it, by gosh. . . .*

Once I had a monkey. A guy in the Bronx sold him to me for seventy-five dollars. I trained him just a little and then took him out on the show just for laughs. He took to it like cool water—in about five minutes the first night my monkey had us eight dollars just by tipping his little hat.

So I had myself an animal act that really paid off. I liked the little son-of-a-gun. Called him Digger. But he got sick with a cold and I sent him home and we lost him. I was sorry. Heck, with that monkey and his hat-tipping business I couldn't miss. We could have been great partners, he and I.

Sure, it gets in your blood. You get so you want the

atmosphere, constant change, the wonderful meeting with the people. And when you're up there with that spiel, you're sitting down and they're all below you and you're the boss of the world.

But I came back. I came home to Abilities and—thank God!—you had a job waiting for me, and I could give up all the carney jazz, the spieling and palm reading and ring tossing and cooch shows, in exchange for something that lasts longer than the popcorn and the pretzels. That's why I came back, Hank. The carney is out of my blood and I have something lasting and real at Abilities. The carney tent is folded up for good; the wanderlust at last is out of my wheels.

27. Halfway

Some individuals, whether disabled or not, are willing to throw all their being, all their strength, into whatever project they face, whatever goal they seek. Hal wanted to work, to live, to find the world's excitement and make it his; and in full measure, he did.

There are other kinds of individuals—found among those who are not disabled as well as those who are—who give not at all or at best only halfway. They pay their taxes and dole out a few pennies to a few charities; they have, they say, "done their bit." There the responsibility ends.

There are those disabled persons who try a little and after the first or second rebuff fall back in despair and defeat. Let the world take care of me, these halfway, half-hearted battlers declare.

I must admit that I have not too much patience or time for the halfway doers, the halfway people, with any who seek to slough off their fellow men—or themselves.

Conversely, those I admire most are those who have accepted this challenge, faced it and triumphed over it. Particularly I mean the wives, the sweethearts, the parents, of the disabled, those among them who give full and unstinting in love, in care, in concern, in effort. There are no more devoted, no more wonderful, no more self-sacrificing people on earth.

Alex's wife, and mine, for example. Art's wife. The parents of Peter. And many of the others we have written of here.

I recall the father of an infant boy with polio, carrying the child in his arms from place to place, office to office, clinic to clinic, seeking a cure for the child. When the boy was grown the father poured his limited savings as a butcher into a new business for his son. When the business failed it did not matter; the father told his son, "I would do the whole thing again if I had the money."

This boy is one of the top executives at Abilities. Much of the lost financial investment he has made up to his father, not only in money but in the victory, the fulfillment, that the father wanted for his son.

Think of the women who have married the badly disabled, the legless, blind, paralyzed—who need love and care. These women are not themselves disabled. They are lovely, full-bodied human beings who give of their love wholly and completely to this husband. This is not the halfway role that seems to do good but only skims the surface, that runs from real trouble—or drives it away.

Halfway people, of whatever category, may do vast harm without even knowing it because they are not willing to go all the way, because they still cringe, because they turn away at the precise moment when turning away may bring heartbreak and defeat.

I think of Barbara, a lovely girl who walks with a kind of springy, swinging motion—a far cry from the strange, contorted gait she used to have. She works on the bench in wiring, and her job is to take a bundle of precut wires and feed them into a small rotating machine. This machine cuts the insulation off the end of each wire, and twists it, and she then takes each wire and dips it in a molten well of solder. This is called skinning, twisting, and dipping. It is not too complicated a business, yet it requires skill and ability, care and intelligence. She has all of these.

She is successful, she is happy, and she is hopeful for her future. Yet there was a time when she was about to be written off forever as a human being, when her life could have been one long dark unturning corridor to nowhere.

For her story, as she told it, is a halfway world from one home to the next, like a game of not-so-musical chairs with a human life as the booby prize.

Until she met at last one that was not halfway.

28. BARBARA: *Party Girl*

I never blamed people or felt angry at them because they did not want me. There has to be a tremendous amount of patience and understanding in dealing with a case like mine, especially the way I was as a very young child. At the start I was in a foundling home and I never knew my own mother was alive until I was fourteen.

The thing I remember most about my earliest childhood is that the people who wanted me, really and truly, were the people I knew in the hospitals, the nurses and the doctors. They were very loving and friendly and I felt that they were a part of me—they were my parents.

The medical term for my condition was cerebral palsy. I was pigeon-toed and knock-kneed. I could not stand without braces and crutches; I had practically no control when I tried to walk, at first, before all the operations.

I was only three when I began undergoing surgery to correct some of this, but my first recollections go back to when I was about five and in the Hospital for Special Surgery.

It was right after that surgery that I went to my first foster home. I'm sure the people there were wonderful, but I was a difficult assignment. I don't remember very much about it. I stayed there a year or two and then I went back into the hospital for four or five more operations to give me more stability, so that at least I could walk in a definite pattern and not fling my legs and arms in any and all directions.

When I was about nine I went to another foster home for a year or two, then it was back to the hospital or the foundling home. I know it was difficult for people to take care of me. Going to school was a problem that wasn't easy for anyone, either. In the hospital there was a teacher who came around but in the home I went to school on the bus. I was pretty good at history and reading, and English—I liked those subjects. But I wasn't any good at math. When I got into high school I was good at algebra but in everyday math I just was no good. The teachers couldn't understand it. Neither can I.

That was the pattern of my childhood. A year—two years—two and a half—in a foster home. Then back to the hospital for surgery. I can't say that any of the people I stayed with were unkind. In the hospital I was accepted, but in the foster homes it often was too much for the parents, especially if they had a child like me, disabled and palsied, who couldn't walk very well and was weak in the legs, the way I was then.

I remember one woman who, after I'd been there two years, said, "Well, you are falling all the time, you are falling down, and I just can't, I just can't——" In other words, I was too much for her. She wanted to do what she could, but taking a badly crippled cerebral palsied child was just too much.

That year I was sent to Camp Oakhurst in New Jersey. It was the first time I had ever been in a place like that, and it was wonderful. I learned how to swim and we sang a lot. Not very well, maybe, but loud.

Only one thing bothered me there, one thing I hadn't bothered about before. No one wrote me letters. When there was mail call and everybody else got something, I just always got nothing. That made me realize for the first time how alone I was.

When I came back from that camp the foundling-home people got me into another foster home temporarily. I was twelve years old and I'd been in about half a dozen homes but I was just too much of a problem for most of them. I had to face that fact. They had to face it. But there was one woman they wanted to try. She had taken in a lot of foster children, and she and her husband were once even Foster Parents of the Year.

The people in the foundling home asked her, "Would you be willing to take on a handicapped?"

She said she didn't know. She hadn't had any experience with severely disabled children; she didn't know if she would be able to do it.

They told her, "Oh, we know you can do it."

She hesitated. "Please take her," the social worker

begged. "Out of nine hundred prospective foster parents nobody will take this little girl, and if someone doesn't, she'll have to go into an institution."

"Well, you can bring her to the house and we'll see."

When I got to this house, the social worker and I, I found something remarkable happening. There was a welcoming party for me. A real party, with the table all set up. There were nine other children in the home, all foster children, and each one of them had a gift for me. It was the most wonderful experience! It was the very first time I'd ever seen Mrs. Brennan or any of those children, and to just walk in and find a party for me, my first party, was the most unexpected thing that had ever happened to me. This wasn't my birthday—besides I'd never had a birthday party either—but there was a cake with candles on it, and everyone sang, "Welcome home, Barbara."

I didn't know any of them, although I had seen some of Mrs. Brennan's "children" before at the foundling home when I was sent back there for physical checkups. I would look at them and think, "Boy, how nice they look and how well they're dressed and everything." It made me feel good to see somebody really dressed nicely like that and I used to dream that someday maybe I'd be there, too. But I never thought I'd really be a part of that family.

Now I was there, just for one day, just for an interview, and the social worker had to take me back to the temporary foster home where I was living. I kept telling myself Mrs. Brennan wouldn't have bothered with the party if she didn't want me, but there were a couple of days, two or three days, when I wasn't sure. Everybody at the foundling home said it would work out, that it was only a matter of red tape. I didn't know for sure, but even if it didn't, I could always remember my party.

Then the social worker came and told me, "You're going to Mrs. Brennan's today, so get everything packed up that you have to take."

Believe me, I was very excited then. I was so happy that I gave the foster mother in the home where I was staying a five-pound box of candy—one of the gifts I'd received at my party. I wanted the foster mother to think I was sad at having to leave. But in my heart I was glad I was going to Mrs. Brennan's. I felt like crying and laughing both at the same time.

When I arrived this second time it was to stay, and Mrs. Brennan had a talk with me, a very serious talk. She explained that in her house everybody is treated the same and everybody goes out and has a good time, because that's the way we should all be, happy, and not sulky or sitting in corners.

I guess she had a good reason for telling me that because I must have been a sulky child. I was always afraid, and I'd always sit in a chair in a corner. She didn't like that. She would come over to me and say, "Come on, Barbara, you've got to go out and play with the others. Why do you want to sit in here by yourself?"

In the other homes I hadn't been allowed to go out and play like that. I sat in one place and that was where I stayed until I was called. That was the way it was, and I had grown used to it until it was just natural to me to find a place and stay there. And it was fear, too, of the way I walked, of the crutches that might slip if I tried to play games. It was a whole lot of fears rolled into one. Sitting in that chair had become my world, my small universe.

After I had been at Mrs. Brennan's she brought in a large doll carriage and loaded it with dolls. "Now, look, Barbara," she told me, "this is for you to play with, but it is also to give you balance, if you want to run around, because with this you won't need crutches."

I stood up and took hold of that doll carriage. Those dolls she had put in there were heavy enough to hold my weight. Right away, I knew, like that. Mrs. Brennan looked back and—"Where's Barbara?" she asked in surprise.

Barbara was outside. Barbara was struggling along with those other children, holding onto that doll carriage. I was running without realizing that I had anything wrong with me or that I had sadness in my mind or heart.

When I met Mr. Brennan, he repeated what his wife had told me, that all the children here have fun and everyone is happy. Then he said, "If there's anything you want, don't be afraid to ask."

That was a brand new idea to me. I had always been afraid to ask anything from anybody. In other places, if I wanted anything, I had to try to find it myself. At the Brennans' I learned what it was like to have a family and to be able to go up and say something without being afraid that I'd get batted or put to bed. That had never happened to me personally, but I knew about it, and I'd learned that it was better to be careful and on guard. But here it was different. Here it was home.

One thing Mrs. Brennan always makes every child

understand—and after me she took in several more disabled foster children—is that everyone has to get along, to learn to love one another. "After all," she says, "when you live under the same roof, you're just like a family, and if you can't get along, what sense is there in having a family?"

That's one of her mottoes. You must love and understand one another, because that is the way God wants it. That is the way she brings all of us up. We go to church, we say grace at meals, we thank God for His goodness and for the fact that we can be a family. When we bring friends into the house we do not say, "This is the foster home where I live. This is Mr. Brennan, this is Mrs. Brennan." We say, "Come in and meet the family. This is my mother, my father. . . ."

It was during this time, just after I started to live here, that I had to go into the hospital again for more surgery, and while I was there I learned by reading some of the medical charts that I had brothers and sisters. The nurse left the charts by my bed one day and I stole a peek at them. And I learned that I had a mother somewhere, too.

In fact, through the foster-home officials, I got to meet some of my sisters, my actual sisters, and I was happy to meet them, though we have drifted apart since. But I was most interested in my mother.

I knew her name, and one time, when I was about sixteen and back in the hospital, I looked up her number in the phone book and called her up.

I asked if she knew who this was calling and she said, "No, I don't."

I said, "Don't you have any children?"

She said, "Yes, several children."

I said, "This is one of them. This is Barbara."

Well, she was really startled, and asked me where I was. I told her I was in the hospital, having my legs fixed and she said, "Well, I hope your legs get better."

I know she wanted to be kind to me but there had been so many worlds and worlds between us that we were strangers. I met one of my aunts, too, and for a time the officials talked about the possibility of my living with her. But when I talked it over, we both knew it wouldn't work out, and so I went back to the Brennans'. I have stayed there with them ever since. I was eleven and a half when I went there for that first birthday party and I am twenty-one now.

Some of us in the family are grown up and still belong and stay there, but, old or young, Mother likes to have us at the dinner table. Then we can go on our merry way on dates or to movies or whatever. The younger ones in the family—she keeps taking in new children—stay at home nights.

Sometimes, often, I stay at home with Mother, too, and look at television. One night we listened to a wonderful man who was appearing on a program with three blind youngsters; he was the president of a company called Abilities out in Albertson, Long Island. That was the first I'd heard of you, Hank.

And I remember I said to mother after the telecast, "Why can't we go out there? Look how nicely he speaks, and how he gives people hope?"

Mother said, "You know, Barbara, maybe that would be a fine thing to do, to go to see this Mr. Viscardi. Maybe he might have something for you."

The very next day, the day after your telecast, we came out and I had my interview. Only a few days later I received a call and Ellen was saying to me, "We want you to come and work at Abilities."

The future—well, I don't know. I have a dream growing in my heart about joining in the work of a convent order, if they would take me. There are orders for the disabled, and for some years I have corresponded with a wonderful nun in Milwaukee. Maybe one day I will go out and talk with her.

I don't know, because there are many questions. I don't know whether they would have me, and whether I would have the strength necessary for such a hard and demanding life. But I would like to do it because I would like to help others as others have helped me.

For I have learned the meaning of love. I have seen it in my home, my family, my mother and father. I have seen it at Abilities in the work that is done here. I know that love is the great healer and that we serve God and Christ when, through care and through concern, we bring love and its meaning and warmth into the lives of others, as it was brought to me at a welcoming party when I was eleven and a half years old.

29. To Love and to Cherish

In the very first chapter, I wrote of the early morning when I came into my office to find Ellen waiting to see me, because she had something to tell me.

She said to me, "I have made up my mind, Mr. Viscardi. I am going to marry Frank."

She said it very simply, and quietly, and irrevocably. But I knew, as she sat before me in that splash of morning sunlight, what was in her heart. I knew the devoutness with which she held her faith, as did Frank also. I knew the torment that both of them had been in for many months because of these things. I knew how much Ellen wanted to be not only a wife to Frank but a mother to his son who was in his custody.

"Ellen," I told her, "I know what you both have gone through—how much you have suffered—and I can only say I want you to be happy. With all my heart I hope you will be. I hope it works out for you. I hope the good Lord will understand."

If I could not condone what she was doing, neither was it my role to sit in judgment. But I could pray with her, and for her happiness and her future.

Ellen knew. And she knew that I understood the long hours of self-searching that must have preceded their decision. But they had suffered too much; they had endured to the limit in physical suffering. They wanted a moment of love in their personal lives.

Ellen asked me, "Mr. Viscardi, will you and your wife be able to come to my wedding? It will be in my apartment in Lynbrook, where we will live after we are married. There will be only one other couple. . . ."

Her eyes were bright as she looked at me.

"Ellen," I told her, "I always said that one day I would weep at your wedding."

Lucile and I would be there because we loved her; because the whole pattern of Abilities is a pattern of love. Without love, without care for the disabled, without concern for what nobody else in the world may be concerned about, there could be no Abilities.

The special quality of what we have to sell is not sentimentality or the corrosive of pity, but love. I am convinced that love is a synonym for motivation, above all in relation to the disabled, but actually in relation to all people, all jobs. There is nothing that we need more—we as individuals—in every phase of life. Love in terms of gratitude, in terms of concern, in terms of opportunity, in terms of acceptance, in terms of teamwork, in terms of responsibility to our neighbors, our brothers, our sons, our daughters. Love in terms of our brotherhood with all mankind.

I cannot but believe that our people at Abilities want to be loved by me and by those they work with. This love is not just a frivolous phrase. It is an unwritten policy of our business, which gives our wonderful, incredible crew a right to share, to know what is going on in the work of which they are part, to understand its problems, to learn new ways in which to do better individually and as a group.

This love I write of is something deeply personal. It is their own awareness of their dignity as human beings, each individually; it is their awareness of their own responsibility to themselves, to their world, their universe, their God; it is their awareness of the right to support themselves rather than be supported. It is love that wants them above all else to fulfill themselves, to be the same, not different from the rest of the world, to be accepted as the ordinary people they really are.

When I was a boy looking at the world from battered stumps I used to dream that one day I would be as others and the words of a poem would run in my thoughts:

> Hold fast your dreams within your heart.
> Keep one still, secret spot where dreams may go
> and sheltered so may thrive and grow where doubt
> and fear are not. . . .

They, these people of Abilities, have kept alive the dream. They have nourished it and made it real and meaningful. Always keep the green dream growing in your heart, however wild and impossible it may appear.

It was in this sense, in these terms, and with this warmth in our hearts that we went to Ellen's wedding.

It was a cloudless, custom-made day for a wedding. Sunlight filled the apartment. Ellen was a wheelchair princess in her attractive, simple beige wedding dress. Frank wore a dark suit which, of course, covered his leg braces. His best man stood at his side.

It was quite a moment in their lives—and ours. I must admit that I fulfilled the promise I had made to Ellen, years back, when her first romance broke up and I assured her that one day I would weep at her wedding. I did. So did my wife, Lucile.

And so, of course, did Ellen.

Afterward, there was champagne and everyone toasted the bride and groom, and Ellen held Frank's son to her with all the love that she has in her heart. And shortly thereafter the newlywed couple departed for their honeymoon, heading south into the sun.

But I know that they did not go completely alone. With them they took also this spirit, this love that reaches out beyond the immediate, this encompassing love which is the foundation of Abilities, of all worthwhile things, all the lasting achievements, all the dazzling moments, in our universe.